50 Sweets Made from Scratch Recipes for Home

By: Kelly Johnson

Table of Contents

- Classic Chocolate Chip Cookies
- Vanilla Cupcakes with Buttercream Frosting
- Fudgy Brownies
- Lemon Bars
- Apple Pie
- Carrot Cake with Cream Cheese Frosting
- Red Velvet Cake
- Blueberry Muffins
- Peanut Butter Cookies
- Strawberry Shortcake
- Chocolate Lava Cake
- Key Lime Pie
- Cinnamon Rolls
- Banana Bread
- Oatmeal Raisin Cookies
- Raspberry Cheesecake
- Pecan Pie
- Tiramisu
- Pineapple Upside-Down Cake
- Almond Biscotti
- Macarons
- Chocolate Truffles
- Coconut Macaroons
- Cherry Cobbler
- Pumpkin Pie
- Cannoli
- Maple Pecan Bars
- Coffee Cake
- S'mores Brownies
- Lemon Meringue Pie
- Gingerbread Cookies
- Peach Crisp
- Snickerdoodles
- Black Forest Cake
- Cranberry Orange Bread
- Eclairs

- Pistachio Baklava
- Peppermint Bark
- Butterscotch Pudding
- Fig Newtons
- German Chocolate Cake
- Rice Krispies Treats
- Mocha Ice Cream
- Raspberry Sorbet
- Orange Creamsicles
- Churros
- Panna Cotta
- Marble Pound Cake
- Bourbon Balls
- Neapolitan Cupcakes

Classic Chocolate Chip Cookies

Ingredients:

- 1 cup (2 sticks) unsalted butter, softened
- 3/4 cup granulated sugar
- 3/4 cup packed brown sugar
- 1 teaspoon vanilla extract
- 2 large eggs
- 2 1/4 cups all-purpose flour
- 1 teaspoon baking soda
- 1/2 teaspoon salt
- 2 cups semisweet chocolate chips

Instructions:

1. Preheat your oven to 375°F (190°C). Line a baking sheet with parchment paper or lightly grease it.
2. In a large mixing bowl, cream together the softened butter, granulated sugar, brown sugar, and vanilla extract until light and fluffy.
3. Beat in the eggs one at a time until well combined.
4. In a separate bowl, whisk together the flour, baking soda, and salt.
5. Gradually add the dry ingredients to the butter mixture, mixing until just combined.
6. Stir in the chocolate chips until evenly distributed throughout the dough.
7. Drop rounded tablespoonfuls of dough onto the prepared baking sheet, spacing them about 2 inches apart.
8. Bake in the preheated oven for 9-11 minutes, or until the edges are golden brown. The centers may still look slightly soft.
9. Remove from the oven and allow the cookies to cool on the baking sheet for 2-3 minutes before transferring them to a wire rack to cool completely.
10. Enjoy your classic chocolate chip cookies with a glass of milk or your favorite hot beverage!

This recipe makes about 3 dozen cookies, depending on the size of your cookie dough scoops. Adjust baking time slightly for softer or crisper cookies, according to your preference.

Vanilla Cupcakes with Buttercream Frosting

Ingredients:

- 1 1/2 cups all-purpose flour
- 1 1/2 teaspoons baking powder
- 1/4 teaspoon salt
- 1/2 cup (1 stick) unsalted butter, softened
- 1 cup granulated sugar
- 2 large eggs, room temperature
- 2 teaspoons vanilla extract
- 1/2 cup milk, room temperature

Instructions:

1. Preheat your oven to 350°F (175°C). Line a muffin tin with cupcake liners.
2. In a medium bowl, whisk together the flour, baking powder, and salt. Set aside.
3. In a large bowl, beat the softened butter and granulated sugar together until light and fluffy, using a hand mixer or a stand mixer fitted with a paddle attachment.
4. Add the eggs one at a time, mixing well after each addition. Add the vanilla extract and mix until combined.
5. Gradually add the dry ingredients to the wet ingredients, alternating with the milk. Begin and end with the dry ingredients, mixing until just combined after each addition. Do not overmix.
6. Fill each cupcake liner about two-thirds full with batter.
7. Bake in the preheated oven for 18-20 minutes, or until a toothpick inserted into the center of a cupcake comes out clean.
8. Remove from the oven and allow the cupcakes to cool in the pan for a few minutes before transferring them to a wire rack to cool completely.

Buttercream Frosting:

Ingredients:

- 1 cup (2 sticks) unsalted butter, softened
- 4 cups powdered sugar
- 1-2 tablespoons heavy cream or milk
- 2 teaspoons vanilla extract
- Pinch of salt (if using unsalted butter)

Instructions:

1. In a large bowl, beat the softened butter with a hand mixer or a stand mixer fitted with a paddle attachment until creamy and smooth.
2. Gradually add the powdered sugar, one cup at a time, mixing on low speed until well blended.

3. Add the vanilla extract, salt (if using), and 1 tablespoon of heavy cream or milk. Beat on medium-high speed for 3-4 minutes until smooth and fluffy. If the frosting is too thick, add more cream or milk, 1 teaspoon at a time, until desired consistency is reached.
4. Once the cupcakes are completely cooled, pipe or spread the buttercream frosting onto each cupcake using a piping bag or a spatula.
5. Decorate with sprinkles, if desired.

Enjoy your homemade vanilla cupcakes with buttercream frosting!

Fudgy Brownies

Ingredients:

- 1 cup (2 sticks) unsalted butter
- 2 cups granulated sugar
- 4 large eggs
- 1 teaspoon vanilla extract
- 3/4 cup unsweetened cocoa powder
- 1 cup all-purpose flour
- 1/2 teaspoon salt
- 1/2 teaspoon baking powder

Instructions:

1. Preheat your oven to 350°F (175°C). Grease a 9x13-inch baking pan or line it with parchment paper.
2. In a medium saucepan, melt the butter over medium heat. Remove from heat and stir in the sugar until well combined.
3. Add the eggs one at a time, mixing well after each addition. Stir in the vanilla extract.
4. In a separate bowl, sift together the cocoa powder, flour, salt, and baking powder.
5. Gradually add the dry ingredients to the butter mixture, mixing until just combined. Do not overmix.
6. Pour the batter into the prepared baking pan and spread it evenly with a spatula.
7. Bake in the preheated oven for 25-30 minutes, or until a toothpick inserted into the center comes out with a few moist crumbs. Be careful not to overbake if you prefer fudgy brownies.
8. Remove from the oven and let the brownies cool completely in the pan on a wire rack.
9. Once cooled, cut into squares and serve. Optionally, dust with powdered sugar or top with a scoop of vanilla ice cream for an extra treat.

These fudgy brownies are sure to satisfy your chocolate cravings with their rich flavor and dense texture. Enjoy baking and indulging in these homemade delights!

Lemon Bars

Ingredients:

For the crust:

- 1 cup (2 sticks) unsalted butter, softened
- 1/2 cup granulated sugar
- 2 cups all-purpose flour
- 1/4 teaspoon salt

For the lemon filling:

- 1 1/2 cups granulated sugar
- 1/4 cup all-purpose flour
- 4 large eggs
- 2/3 cup freshly squeezed lemon juice (from about 4-5 lemons)
- Zest of 1 lemon
- Powdered sugar, for dusting

Instructions:

1. **Preheat** your oven to 350°F (175°C). Grease a 9x13-inch baking pan or line it with parchment paper, leaving some overhang for easy removal.
2. **Make the crust:** In a large bowl, cream together the softened butter and granulated sugar until light and fluffy. Gradually add the flour and salt, mixing until the dough comes together and forms a crumbly mixture.
3. **Press the crust:** Press the crust mixture evenly into the bottom of the prepared baking pan. You can use your hands or the back of a spoon to press it down firmly.
4. **Bake the crust:** Bake the crust in the preheated oven for 20-25 minutes, or until lightly golden brown.
5. **Prepare the lemon filling:** While the crust is baking, make the lemon filling. In a medium bowl, whisk together the granulated sugar and flour. Add the eggs, lemon juice, and lemon zest, and whisk until smooth and well combined.
6. **Pour over the crust:** Pour the lemon filling over the hot crust immediately after removing it from the oven.
7. **Bake again:** Return the pan to the oven and bake for an additional 20-25 minutes, or until the filling is set and no longer jiggles when gently shaken.
8. **Cool and chill:** Remove the pan from the oven and let the lemon bars cool completely in the pan on a wire rack. Once cooled, refrigerate for at least 1-2 hours to chill and set the filling.
9. **Cut and serve:** Once chilled, lift the lemon bars out of the pan using the parchment paper overhang. Dust with powdered sugar. Cut into squares or bars using a sharp knife, wiping the knife clean between cuts for neat edges.
10. **Enjoy!** Serve these refreshing lemon bars as a delightful dessert or snack.

These lemon bars are perfect for citrus lovers and make a wonderful treat for any occasion. The combination of tangy lemon and buttery crust is sure to be a hit

Apple Pie

Ingredients:

For the pie crust:

- 2 1/2 cups all-purpose flour
- 1 teaspoon salt
- 1 tablespoon granulated sugar
- 1 cup (2 sticks) unsalted butter, cold and cut into small cubes
- 6-8 tablespoons ice water

For the apple filling:

- 6-7 cups thinly sliced apples (about 6-7 medium-sized apples, such as Granny Smith, Honeycrisp, or a mix)
- 1/2 cup granulated sugar
- 1/4 cup packed light brown sugar
- 1 tablespoon lemon juice
- 1 teaspoon ground cinnamon
- 1/4 teaspoon ground nutmeg
- 1/4 teaspoon salt
- 2 tablespoons unsalted butter, cut into small pieces

For assembling and finishing:

- 1 egg, beaten (for egg wash)
- 1 tablespoon granulated sugar (for sprinkling on top)

Instructions:

1. **Make the pie crust:**
    - In a large bowl, whisk together the flour, salt, and sugar.
    - Add the cold cubed butter to the flour mixture. Use a pastry cutter or your fingers to cut the butter into the flour until the mixture resembles coarse crumbs with pea-sized pieces of butter.
    - Gradually add the ice water, 1 tablespoon at a time, mixing with a fork or your hands until the dough just begins to come together. Be careful not to overwork the dough.
    - Divide the dough in half, shape each half into a flat disc, wrap them tightly in plastic wrap, and refrigerate for at least 1 hour (or up to 2 days).
2. **Prepare the apple filling:**
    - In a large bowl, combine the thinly sliced apples, granulated sugar, brown sugar, lemon juice, cinnamon, nutmeg, and salt. Toss until the apples are evenly coated.
3. **Assemble the pie:**

- Preheat your oven to 400°F (200°C) and place a baking sheet on the middle rack to catch any drips.
- On a lightly floured surface, roll out one disc of chilled dough into a circle about 12 inches in diameter. Carefully transfer it to a 9-inch pie dish, gently pressing it into the bottom and sides.
- Pour the apple filling into the prepared pie crust, spreading it out evenly. Dot the filling with small pieces of butter.

4. **Top the pie:**
   - Roll out the second disc of chilled dough into a circle about 12 inches in diameter. You can leave it whole to make a traditional double-crust pie, or cut it into strips to make a lattice crust.
   - If making a double-crust pie, place the rolled-out dough over the apple filling. Trim any excess dough hanging over the edges and crimp the edges to seal. Cut slits in the top crust to allow steam to escape.
   - If making a lattice crust, cut the rolled-out dough into strips and arrange them in a lattice pattern over the apple filling. Trim any excess dough hanging over the edges and press the edges to seal.

5. **Bake the pie:**
   - Brush the top crust with the beaten egg and sprinkle with granulated sugar for a golden finish.
   - Place the pie on the preheated baking sheet in the oven. Bake for 45-55 minutes, or until the crust is golden brown and the filling is bubbling.
   - If the edges of the crust start to brown too quickly, cover them loosely with foil.

6. **Cool and serve:**
   - Remove the pie from the oven and let it cool on a wire rack for at least 2 hours before slicing and serving. This allows the filling to set.

7. **Enjoy!** Serve slices of apple pie warm or at room temperature, optionally with a scoop of vanilla ice cream or a dollop of whipped cream.

This homemade apple pie is sure to be a hit with its buttery crust and flavorful apple filling. It's a comforting dessert that's perfect for sharing with family and friends!

Carrot Cake with Cream Cheese Frosting

Ingredients:

For the carrot cake:

- 2 cups all-purpose flour
- 2 teaspoons baking powder
- 1 1/2 teaspoons baking soda
- 1/2 teaspoon salt
- 1 teaspoon ground cinnamon
- 1/2 teaspoon ground nutmeg
- 1 cup vegetable oil
- 1 cup granulated sugar
- 1 cup packed light brown sugar
- 4 large eggs
- 2 teaspoons vanilla extract
- 3 cups grated carrots (about 4-5 medium carrots)
- 1 cup chopped nuts (optional, such as walnuts or pecans)
- 1/2 cup crushed pineapple, drained (optional)

For the cream cheese frosting:

- 8 oz (1 package) cream cheese, softened
- 1/2 cup (1 stick) unsalted butter, softened
- 4 cups powdered sugar
- 1 teaspoon vanilla extract
- Pinch of salt

Instructions:

1. **Preheat** your oven to 350°F (175°C). Grease and flour two 9-inch round cake pans, or line them with parchment paper for easier removal.
2. **Make the carrot cake:**
    - In a medium bowl, whisk together the flour, baking powder, baking soda, salt, cinnamon, and nutmeg. Set aside.
    - In a large bowl, whisk together the vegetable oil, granulated sugar, brown sugar, eggs, and vanilla extract until well combined and smooth.
    - Gradually add the dry ingredients to the wet ingredients, mixing until just combined.
    - Fold in the grated carrots, chopped nuts (if using), and crushed pineapple (if using) until evenly distributed in the batter.
3. **Bake the cake:**
    - Divide the batter evenly between the prepared cake pans.

- Bake in the preheated oven for 30-35 minutes, or until a toothpick inserted into the center comes out clean.
- Remove from the oven and allow the cakes to cool in the pans for 10 minutes before transferring them to a wire rack to cool completely.

4. **Make the cream cheese frosting:**
   - In a large bowl, beat the softened cream cheese and butter together until smooth and creamy.
   - Gradually add the powdered sugar, one cup at a time, mixing on low speed until well blended.
   - Add the vanilla extract and a pinch of salt, and beat on medium-high speed for 2-3 minutes until the frosting is light and fluffy.

5. **Assemble the cake:**
   - Once the cake layers are completely cool, place one layer on a serving plate or cake stand.
   - Spread a generous layer of cream cheese frosting over the top of the first layer.
   - Place the second cake layer on top and spread the remaining frosting over the top and sides of the cake.
   - Optionally, decorate the top with chopped nuts or a sprinkle of cinnamon.

6. **Chill (optional):**
   - For easier slicing, you can chill the cake in the refrigerator for 30 minutes to 1 hour before serving.

7. **Serve and enjoy!** Carrot cake with cream cheese frosting is best served at room temperature. Slice and enjoy this moist and flavorful dessert with a cup of tea or coffee.

This homemade carrot cake with cream cheese frosting is sure to be a crowd-pleaser with its moist texture, sweet carrots, and tangy frosting. Perfect for celebrations or as a special treat any day!

Red Velvet Cake

Ingredients:

For the cake:

- 2 1/2 cups all-purpose flour
- 1 1/2 cups granulated sugar
- 1 teaspoon baking soda
- 1 teaspoon salt
- 1 teaspoon cocoa powder
- 1 1/2 cups vegetable oil
- 1 cup buttermilk, room temperature
- 2 large eggs, room temperature
- 2 tablespoons red food coloring
- 1 teaspoon vanilla extract
- 1 teaspoon white vinegar

For the cream cheese frosting:

- 16 oz (2 packages) cream cheese, softened
- 1 cup (2 sticks) unsalted butter, softened
- 4 cups powdered sugar
- 1 teaspoon vanilla extract
- Pinch of salt

Instructions:

1. **Preheat** your oven to 350°F (175°C). Grease and flour two 9-inch round cake pans, or line them with parchment paper.
2. **Make the cake:**
    - In a large bowl, sift together the flour, sugar, baking soda, salt, and cocoa powder. Set aside.
    - In another large bowl or the bowl of a stand mixer, whisk together the vegetable oil, buttermilk, eggs, red food coloring, vanilla extract, and white vinegar until well combined.
    - Gradually add the dry ingredients to the wet ingredients, mixing on low speed until just combined and smooth. Be careful not to overmix.
3. **Bake the cake:**
    - Divide the batter evenly between the prepared cake pans.
    - Bake in the preheated oven for 25-30 minutes, or until a toothpick inserted into the center comes out clean.
    - Remove from the oven and let the cakes cool in the pans for 10 minutes before transferring them to a wire rack to cool completely.
4. **Make the cream cheese frosting:**

- In a large bowl, beat the softened cream cheese and butter together until smooth and creamy.
- Gradually add the powdered sugar, one cup at a time, mixing on low speed until well blended.
- Add the vanilla extract and a pinch of salt, and beat on medium-high speed for 2-3 minutes until the frosting is light and fluffy.

5. **Assemble the cake:**
    - Once the cake layers are completely cool, place one layer on a serving plate or cake stand.
    - Spread a layer of cream cheese frosting over the top of the first layer.
    - Place the second cake layer on top and spread the remaining frosting over the top and sides of the cake.
    - Optionally, use a spatula or knife to create decorative swirls on the frosting.
6. **Chill (optional):**
    - For easier slicing and to let the flavors meld, you can chill the cake in the refrigerator for 30 minutes to 1 hour before serving.
7. **Serve and enjoy!** Red velvet cake is best served at room temperature. Slice and enjoy this decadent and visually stunning dessert.

This homemade red velvet cake with cream cheese frosting is sure to impress with its vibrant color and delicious flavor. Perfect for birthdays, holidays, or any special occasion!

Blueberry Muffins

Ingredients:

- 2 cups all-purpose flour
- 1 tablespoon baking powder
- 1/2 teaspoon salt
- 1/2 cup (1 stick) unsalted butter, melted and cooled slightly
- 1 cup granulated sugar
- 2 large eggs
- 1 cup milk (whole milk or buttermilk)
- 1 teaspoon vanilla extract
- 1 1/2 cups fresh or frozen blueberries (if using frozen, do not thaw)

Instructions:

1. **Preheat** your oven to 375°F (190°C). Line a muffin tin with paper liners or grease the wells with butter or cooking spray.
2. **Prepare the dry ingredients:**
   - In a large bowl, whisk together the flour, baking powder, and salt. Set aside.
3. **Prepare the wet ingredients:**
   - In another bowl, whisk together the melted butter and granulated sugar until well combined.
   - Add the eggs one at a time, whisking well after each addition.
   - Whisk in the milk and vanilla extract until smooth.
4. **Combine wet and dry ingredients:**
   - Pour the wet ingredients into the bowl with the dry ingredients. Use a spatula or wooden spoon to gently fold the mixture together until just combined. Do not overmix; it's okay if there are a few lumps.
5. **Fold in the blueberries:**
   - Gently fold the blueberries into the batter. If using frozen blueberries, be careful not to overmix to avoid discoloring the batter.
6. **Fill the muffin tin:**
   - Divide the batter evenly among the muffin cups, filling each about 3/4 full.
7. **Bake the muffins:**
   - Bake in the preheated oven for 18-20 minutes, or until the tops are golden brown and a toothpick inserted into the center of a muffin comes out clean.
8. **Cool and serve:**
   - Remove the muffin tin from the oven and let the muffins cool in the tin for 5 minutes.
   - Transfer the muffins to a wire rack to cool completely, or serve warm.
9. **Enjoy!** These blueberry muffins are best enjoyed fresh on the day they are baked. Store any leftovers in an airtight container at room temperature for up to 2 days, or freeze for longer storage.

These homemade blueberry muffins are moist, fluffy, and packed with bursts of fruity flavor from the blueberries. They are perfect for breakfast, brunch, or as a snack any time of the day!

Peanut Butter Cookies

Ingredients:

- 1/2 cup (1 stick) unsalted butter, softened
- 1/2 cup creamy peanut butter
- 1/2 cup granulated sugar
- 1/2 cup packed light brown sugar
- 1 large egg
- 1 teaspoon vanilla extract
- 1 1/4 cups all-purpose flour
- 1/2 teaspoon baking powder
- 1/2 teaspoon baking soda
- 1/4 teaspoon salt

Instructions:

1. **Preheat** your oven to 350°F (175°C). Line a baking sheet with parchment paper or lightly grease it.
2. **Cream butter, peanut butter, and sugars:**
    - In a large bowl, beat together the softened butter, creamy peanut butter, granulated sugar, and brown sugar until smooth and creamy.
3. **Add egg and vanilla:**
    - Beat in the egg and vanilla extract until well combined.
4. **Combine dry ingredients:**
    - In a separate bowl, whisk together the flour, baking powder, baking soda, and salt.
5. **Mix wet and dry ingredients:**
    - Gradually add the dry ingredients to the wet ingredients, mixing until just combined. Be careful not to overmix.
6. **Form cookie dough balls:**
    - Roll the dough into balls, about 1 tablespoon each, and place them 2 inches apart on the prepared baking sheet. You can use a fork to make a criss-cross pattern on top of each cookie, pressing down slightly.
7. **Bake the cookies:**
    - Bake in the preheated oven for 10-12 minutes, or until the edges are lightly golden brown.
8. **Cool and enjoy:**
    - Remove from the oven and let the cookies cool on the baking sheet for a few minutes before transferring them to a wire rack to cool completely.
9. **Store:**
    - Store the cooled cookies in an airtight container at room temperature for up to one week.

These peanut butter cookies are soft and chewy with a delicious peanut butter flavor. They are perfect for enjoying with a glass of milk or sharing with friends and family!

Strawberry Shortcake

Ingredients:

For the shortcake:

- 2 cups all-purpose flour
- 1/4 cup granulated sugar
- 1 tablespoon baking powder
- 1/2 teaspoon salt
- 1/2 cup (1 stick) unsalted butter, cold and cut into small pieces
- 1 large egg
- 2/3 cup heavy cream
- 1 teaspoon vanilla extract

For the strawberries:

- 1 pound fresh strawberries, hulled and sliced
- 2-3 tablespoons granulated sugar (adjust to taste)

For the whipped cream:

- 1 cup heavy cream, chilled
- 2 tablespoons powdered sugar
- 1 teaspoon vanilla extract

Instructions:

1. **Preheat** your oven to 400°F (200°C). Line a baking sheet with parchment paper or lightly grease it.
2. **Prepare the shortcake:**
    - In a large bowl, whisk together the flour, sugar, baking powder, and salt.
    - Cut in the cold butter using a pastry cutter or your fingers until the mixture resembles coarse crumbs.
    - In a small bowl, whisk together the egg, heavy cream, and vanilla extract.
    - Gradually add the wet ingredients to the dry ingredients, stirring with a fork until the dough just comes together.
3. **Shape the shortcake:**
    - Turn the dough out onto a lightly floured surface and gently knead it a few times until it holds together.
    - Pat the dough into a circle about 1-inch thick. Use a round biscuit cutter or a glass to cut out rounds of dough, about 3 inches in diameter.
    - Place the rounds on the prepared baking sheet, spacing them about 2 inches apart.
4. **Bake the shortcakes:**

- Bake in the preheated oven for 15-18 minutes, or until the tops are golden brown. Remove from the oven and let them cool slightly on the baking sheet before transferring to a wire rack to cool completely.
5. **Prepare the strawberries:**
    - In a medium bowl, toss the sliced strawberries with granulated sugar to taste. Let them sit for about 15-20 minutes to allow the strawberries to release their juices.
6. **Make the whipped cream:**
    - In a chilled bowl, whip the heavy cream, powdered sugar, and vanilla extract together until soft peaks form.
7. **Assemble the strawberry shortcakes:**
    - To serve, slice each cooled shortcake in half horizontally.
    - Place a spoonful of strawberries on the bottom half of each shortcake, followed by a dollop of whipped cream.
    - Place the top half of the shortcake over the whipped cream.
    - Garnish with additional strawberries and a dusting of powdered sugar, if desired.
8. **Serve and enjoy!** Strawberry shortcake is best served immediately while the shortcakes are still slightly warm and the strawberries are juicy.

This homemade strawberry shortcake is a delightful summer dessert that highlights the natural sweetness of strawberries and the buttery richness of the shortcake. It's perfect for picnics, parties, or any occasion!

Chocolate Lava Cake

Ingredients:

- 1/2 cup (1 stick) unsalted butter
- 8 oz (about 1 1/3 cups) semi-sweet or bittersweet chocolate, chopped
- 1/4 cup granulated sugar
- 1/4 teaspoon salt
- 4 large eggs
- 4 large egg yolks
- 2 teaspoons vanilla extract
- 1/4 cup all-purpose flour
- Optional: Powdered sugar or cocoa powder, for dusting
- Optional: Vanilla ice cream or whipped cream, for serving

Instructions:

1. **Preheat** your oven to 425°F (220°C). Grease and lightly flour four 6-ounce ramekins or custard cups. Place them on a baking sheet for easier handling.
2. **Melt butter and chocolate:**
   - In a medium heatproof bowl set over a pot of simmering water (double boiler method) or in the microwave in short bursts, melt the butter and chopped chocolate together until smooth and well combined. Stir occasionally. Remove from heat and let cool slightly.
3. **Prepare the batter:**
   - In a large bowl, whisk together the granulated sugar, salt, eggs, egg yolks, and vanilla extract until well combined.
   - Gradually whisk in the melted chocolate mixture until smooth.
   - Sift the flour over the batter and gently fold it in until just combined. Be careful not to overmix.
4. **Fill the ramekins:**
   - Divide the batter evenly among the prepared ramekins, filling them about 3/4 full.
5. **Bake the lava cakes:**
   - Place the baking sheet with the filled ramekins in the preheated oven.
   - Bake for 12-14 minutes, or until the edges are set but the center still looks soft.
6. **Serve:**
   - Remove the lava cakes from the oven and let them cool in the ramekins for 1-2 minutes.
   - Carefully invert each cake onto a dessert plate. If desired, dust with powdered sugar or cocoa powder.
   - Serve immediately while warm, with a scoop of vanilla ice cream or a dollop of whipped cream if desired.
7. **Enjoy!** Break into the molten center with a spoon and enjoy the rich, gooey chocolate goodness of these lava cakes.

These chocolate lava cakes are perfect for a special occasion or a romantic dessert at home. They are sure to impress with their melt-in-your-mouth texture and intense chocolate flavor!

Key Lime Pie

Ingredients:

For the crust:

- 1 1/2 cups graham cracker crumbs (about 10-12 whole graham crackers)
- 1/3 cup granulated sugar
- 6 tablespoons unsalted butter, melted

For the filling:

- 4 large egg yolks
- 14 oz (1 can) sweetened condensed milk
- 1/2 cup key lime juice (freshly squeezed if possible)
- 1 tablespoon finely grated key lime zest (optional, for extra flavor)

For the whipped cream topping:

- 1 cup heavy cream, chilled
- 2 tablespoons powdered sugar
- 1/2 teaspoon vanilla extract

Instructions:

1. **Preheat** your oven to 350°F (175°C).
2. **Make the crust:**
    - In a medium bowl, combine the graham cracker crumbs and granulated sugar.
    - Add the melted butter and stir until the mixture resembles coarse sand and holds together when pressed.
    - Press the mixture firmly and evenly into the bottom and up the sides of a 9-inch pie dish.
    - Bake the crust in the preheated oven for 10 minutes. Remove and let it cool slightly while preparing the filling.
3. **Make the filling:**
    - In a large bowl, whisk the egg yolks until smooth and creamy.
    - Add the sweetened condensed milk and whisk until well combined.
    - Gradually whisk in the key lime juice and key lime zest (if using) until smooth and slightly thickened.
4. **Bake the pie:**
    - Pour the filling into the pre-baked graham cracker crust.
    - Return the pie to the oven and bake for 15 minutes, or until the filling is set but still slightly jiggly in the center.
    - Remove from the oven and let the pie cool to room temperature on a wire rack. Then refrigerate for at least 2 hours, or until thoroughly chilled and set.
5. **Make the whipped cream topping:**

- In a chilled bowl, whip the heavy cream, powdered sugar, and vanilla extract together until soft peaks form.
6. **Serve:**
    - Spread or pipe the whipped cream over the chilled key lime pie before serving.
    - Optionally, garnish with additional key lime zest or slices for decoration.
7. **Enjoy!** Slice and serve this tangy and creamy key lime pie as a refreshing dessert after a meal.

This homemade key lime pie is bursting with citrus flavor and has a perfect balance of sweet and tart. It's a wonderful dessert for any occasion, especially during the warmer months!

Cinnamon Rolls

Ingredients:

For the dough:

- 1 cup warm milk (about 110°F)
- 2 1/4 teaspoons active dry yeast (1 packet)
- 1/2 cup granulated sugar
- 1/3 cup unsalted butter, melted
- 2 large eggs
- 1 teaspoon salt
- 4 1/2 cups all-purpose flour, plus more for dusting

For the filling:

- 1 cup packed light brown sugar
- 2 1/2 tablespoons ground cinnamon
- 1/3 cup unsalted butter, softened

For the icing:

- 4 oz cream cheese, softened
- 1/4 cup unsalted butter, softened
- 1 cup powdered sugar
- 1/2 teaspoon vanilla extract
- Pinch of salt

Instructions:

1. **Activate the yeast:**
   - In a small bowl, dissolve the yeast in the warm milk. Let it sit for about 5-10 minutes until foamy.
2. **Make the dough:**
   - In a large bowl or the bowl of a stand mixer fitted with a dough hook, combine the yeast mixture, sugar, melted butter, eggs, salt, and 4 cups of flour. Mix until smooth.
   - Gradually add the remaining 1/2 cup of flour, kneading until the dough is smooth and elastic, about 5-7 minutes. The dough should be slightly sticky but manageable.
   - Transfer the dough to a lightly greased bowl, cover with plastic wrap or a clean kitchen towel, and let it rise in a warm place until doubled in size, about 1-2 hours.
3. **Make the filling:**
   - In a small bowl, mix together the brown sugar and cinnamon for the filling.
4. **Roll out the dough:**

- Once the dough has doubled in size, punch it down and roll it out on a lightly floured surface into a large rectangle, about 16x21 inches.
- Spread the softened butter evenly over the dough, leaving a small border around the edges.
- Sprinkle the cinnamon-sugar mixture over the buttered dough.
5. **Roll and cut the cinnamon rolls:**
    - Starting from one long edge, tightly roll up the dough into a log.
    - Use a sharp knife to cut the log into 12 equal slices.
6. **Arrange in a pan:**
    - Place the cinnamon rolls in a greased 9x13-inch baking pan or two 9-inch round cake pans, with the cut side facing upwards. Space them evenly in the pan(s).
7. **Rise again:**
    - Cover the rolls loosely with plastic wrap or a clean kitchen towel and let them rise in a warm place for another 30-45 minutes, until puffy and nearly doubled in size.
8. **Bake the cinnamon rolls:**
    - Preheat your oven to 350°F (175°C). Bake the rolls for 20-25 minutes, or until golden brown.
9. **Make the icing:**
    - While the rolls are baking, prepare the icing. In a medium bowl, beat together the softened cream cheese and butter until smooth.
    - Add the powdered sugar, vanilla extract, and salt, and beat until creamy and smooth.
10. **Ice the rolls:**
    - Spread the icing over the warm cinnamon rolls as soon as they come out of the oven, allowing it to melt into the rolls.
11. **Serve and enjoy!** These homemade cinnamon rolls are best served warm. Pull apart and enjoy the gooey cinnamon goodness with a cup of coffee or tea.

These cinnamon rolls are sure to be a hit with their soft, fluffy texture and delicious cinnamon filling. Perfect for a special breakfast or brunch treat!

Banana Bread

Ingredients:

- 2 to 3 ripe bananas, mashed (about 1 cup)
- 1/3 cup unsalted butter, melted
- 3/4 cup granulated sugar
- 1 large egg, beaten
- 1 teaspoon vanilla extract
- 1 teaspoon baking soda
- Pinch of salt
- 1 1/2 cups all-purpose flour

Optional add-ins:

- 1/2 cup chopped nuts (such as walnuts or pecans)
- 1/2 cup chocolate chips

Instructions:

1. **Preheat** your oven to 350°F (175°C). Grease a 9x5-inch loaf pan or line it with parchment paper.
2. **Mix wet ingredients:**
   - In a mixing bowl, mash the ripe bananas with a fork or potato masher until smooth.
   - Stir in the melted butter.
3. **Add sugar, egg, and vanilla:**
   - Add the granulated sugar, beaten egg, and vanilla extract to the banana mixture. Stir until well combined.
4. **Incorporate dry ingredients:**
   - Sprinkle the baking soda and salt over the banana mixture and stir to combine.
   - Gently fold in the flour until just incorporated. Be careful not to overmix; a few lumps are okay.
5. **Optional add-ins:**
   - If using, fold in chopped nuts or chocolate chips at this point.
6. **Bake:**
   - Pour the batter into the prepared loaf pan and spread it out evenly.
   - Bake in the preheated oven for 60-65 minutes, or until a toothpick inserted into the center comes out clean.
7. **Cool and serve:**
   - Remove the banana bread from the oven and let it cool in the pan for 10 minutes.
   - Transfer the bread to a wire rack to cool completely before slicing.
8. **Enjoy!** Slice and enjoy this delicious banana bread warm or at room temperature. It's perfect for breakfast, as a snack, or anytime you crave a comforting treat.

This homemade banana bread is moist, flavorful, and a great way to use up ripe bananas. It can be customized with nuts, chocolate chips, or even a swirl of peanut butter for extra indulgence!

Oatmeal Raisin Cookies

Ingredients:

- 1 cup (2 sticks) unsalted butter, softened
- 1 cup packed light brown sugar
- 1/2 cup granulated sugar
- 2 large eggs
- 1 teaspoon vanilla extract
- 1 1/2 cups all-purpose flour
- 1 teaspoon baking soda
- 1 teaspoon ground cinnamon
- 1/2 teaspoon salt
- 3 cups old-fashioned rolled oats
- 1 cup raisins (or chopped dried cranberries)

Instructions:

1. **Preheat** your oven to 350°F (175°C). Line a baking sheet with parchment paper or lightly grease it.
2. **Cream butter and sugars:**
   - In a large bowl, beat together the softened butter, brown sugar, and granulated sugar until light and fluffy.
3. **Add eggs and vanilla:**
   - Beat in the eggs, one at a time, until well combined.
   - Add the vanilla extract and mix until smooth.
4. **Combine dry ingredients:**
   - In a separate bowl, whisk together the flour, baking soda, cinnamon, and salt.
5. **Mix wet and dry ingredients:**
   - Gradually add the dry ingredients to the wet ingredients, mixing until just combined.
   - Stir in the rolled oats and raisins until evenly distributed in the dough.
6. **Chill the dough (optional):**
   - For thicker cookies, you can chill the dough in the refrigerator for 30 minutes to 1 hour.
7. **Form cookie dough balls:**
   - Drop rounded tablespoons of dough onto the prepared baking sheet, spacing them about 2 inches apart.
8. **Bake the cookies:**
   - Bake in the preheated oven for 10-12 minutes, or until the edges are lightly golden brown.
9. **Cool and enjoy:**
   - Remove from the oven and let the cookies cool on the baking sheet for 5 minutes before transferring them to a wire rack to cool completely.

10. **Serve and enjoy!** These oatmeal raisin cookies are best enjoyed warm or at room temperature with a glass of milk or your favorite hot beverage.

These homemade oatmeal raisin cookies are chewy, flavorful, and perfect for sharing with family and friends. They store well in an airtight container for several days, although they're often enjoyed fresh out of the oven!

Raspberry Cheesecake

Ingredients:

For the crust:

- 1 1/2 cups graham cracker crumbs (about 10-12 whole graham crackers)
- 1/4 cup granulated sugar
- 1/2 cup unsalted butter, melted

For the cheesecake filling:

- 24 oz (3 packages) cream cheese, softened
- 1 cup granulated sugar
- 3 large eggs
- 1 cup sour cream
- 1 teaspoon vanilla extract
- 1/4 cup all-purpose flour

For the raspberry swirl:

- 1 cup fresh raspberries (or thawed frozen raspberries)
- 2 tablespoons granulated sugar
- 1 tablespoon water
- 1 teaspoon cornstarch

Instructions:

1. **Preheat** your oven to 325°F (160°C). Grease a 9-inch springform pan and line the bottom with parchment paper.
2. **Make the crust:**
    - In a medium bowl, combine the graham cracker crumbs, granulated sugar, and melted butter. Stir until the mixture resembles wet sand.
    - Press the mixture firmly into the bottom of the prepared springform pan. Use the back of a spoon or a flat-bottomed glass to compact it evenly.
3. **Prepare the raspberry swirl:**
    - In a small saucepan, combine the raspberries, granulated sugar, water, and cornstarch.
    - Cook over medium heat, stirring constantly, until the mixture thickens and the raspberries break down, about 5-7 minutes.
    - Remove from heat and strain through a fine mesh sieve to remove the seeds. Set aside to cool.
4. **Make the cheesecake filling:**
    - In a large bowl or the bowl of a stand mixer fitted with the paddle attachment, beat the softened cream cheese until smooth and creamy.
    - Add the granulated sugar and beat until well combined.

- Add the eggs one at a time, mixing well after each addition.
- Mix in the sour cream and vanilla extract until smooth.
- Gradually add the flour and mix until just combined, being careful not to overmix.

5. **Assemble the cheesecake:**
    - Pour the cheesecake filling over the prepared crust in the springform pan.
    - Spoon dollops of the raspberry sauce over the top of the cheesecake filling.
    - Use a knife or skewer to gently swirl the raspberry sauce into the cheesecake batter to create a marbled effect.
6. **Bake the cheesecake:**
    - Place the springform pan on a baking sheet (to catch any potential leaks) and bake in the preheated oven for 50-60 minutes, or until the edges are set and the center is slightly jiggly.
7. **Cool and chill:**
    - Remove the cheesecake from the oven and let it cool in the pan on a wire rack for 1 hour.
    - Cover the cheesecake with plastic wrap and refrigerate for at least 4 hours, preferably overnight, to set.
8. **Serve:**
    - Before serving, release the cheesecake from the springform pan. Slice and serve chilled.
9. **Enjoy!** This raspberry cheesecake is creamy, tangy, and bursting with raspberry flavor, making it a perfect dessert for any occasion.

This homemade raspberry cheesecake is sure to impress with its beautiful marbled appearance and decadent taste. It's a wonderful treat to share with friends and family!

Pecan Pie

Ingredients:

For the pie crust:

- 1 1/4 cups all-purpose flour
- 1/2 teaspoon salt
- 1/2 teaspoon granulated sugar
- 1/2 cup (1 stick) unsalted butter, cold and cut into small pieces
- 3-4 tablespoons ice water

For the filling:

- 1 cup granulated sugar
- 3/4 cup light corn syrup
- 1/2 cup unsalted butter, melted and slightly cooled
- 3 large eggs, lightly beaten
- 1 teaspoon vanilla extract
- 1/4 teaspoon salt
- 1 1/2 cups pecan halves

Instructions:

1. **Make the pie crust:**
    - In a large bowl, whisk together the flour, salt, and sugar.
    - Add the cold butter pieces and cut them into the flour mixture using a pastry cutter or your fingers, until the mixture resembles coarse crumbs.
    - Gradually add the ice water, 1 tablespoon at a time, mixing with a fork until the dough just begins to come together.
    - Shape the dough into a ball, flatten into a disk, wrap tightly in plastic wrap, and refrigerate for at least 1 hour.
2. **Prepare the crust:**
    - On a lightly floured surface, roll out the chilled dough into a circle about 12 inches in diameter.
    - Carefully transfer the dough to a 9-inch pie dish. Trim any excess dough from the edges and crimp as desired. Refrigerate the crust while preparing the filling.
3. **Preheat** your oven to 350°F (175°C).
4. **Make the filling:**
    - In a large bowl, whisk together the granulated sugar, corn syrup, melted butter, eggs, vanilla extract, and salt until well combined.
    - Stir in the pecan halves.
5. **Assemble and bake the pie:**
    - Pour the filling into the chilled pie crust, spreading the pecans evenly.

- Place the pie on a baking sheet to catch any spills and bake in the preheated oven for 50-60 minutes, or until the filling is set and the crust is golden brown.
6. **Cool and serve:**
    - Remove the pie from the oven and let it cool completely on a wire rack before slicing and serving.
7. **Enjoy!** Serve slices of pecan pie at room temperature or slightly warmed, optionally topped with whipped cream or vanilla ice cream.

This homemade pecan pie is decadent, sweet, and nutty, with a buttery crust that complements the rich filling perfectly. It's a perfect dessert for holidays or any special occasion!

Tiramisu

Ingredients:

- 1 cup strong brewed coffee or espresso, cooled to room temperature
- 2 tablespoons coffee liqueur (such as Kahlua), optional
- 3 large egg yolks
- 1/2 cup granulated sugar
- 1 cup mascarpone cheese, room temperature
- 1 cup heavy cream
- 1 teaspoon vanilla extract
- 24-30 ladyfinger biscuits (savoiardi)
- Unsweetened cocoa powder, for dusting

Instructions:

1. **Brew the coffee:**
   - Prepare 1 cup of strong coffee or espresso. Let it cool to room temperature. If using, stir in the coffee liqueur.
2. **Prepare the mascarpone cream:**
   - In a large mixing bowl, whisk together the egg yolks and granulated sugar until pale and creamy.
3. **Add mascarpone cheese:**
   - Add the mascarpone cheese to the egg yolk mixture and beat until smooth and well combined.
4. **Whip the cream:**
   - In a separate bowl, whip the heavy cream and vanilla extract until stiff peaks form.
5. **Combine mascarpone mixture and whipped cream:**
   - Gently fold the whipped cream into the mascarpone mixture until smooth and creamy. Be careful not to overmix.
6. **Assemble the tiramisu:**
   - Dip each ladyfinger biscuit into the coffee mixture for about 1-2 seconds on each side, allowing them to absorb some coffee without becoming too soggy.
   - Arrange a layer of soaked ladyfingers in the bottom of a 9x9-inch square dish or a similar-sized serving dish.
   - Spread half of the mascarpone cream mixture evenly over the ladyfingers.
7. **Repeat layers:**
   - Repeat with another layer of soaked ladyfingers and the remaining mascarpone cream mixture.
8. **Chill:**
   - Cover the tiramisu with plastic wrap and refrigerate for at least 4 hours, preferably overnight, to allow the flavors to meld and the dessert to set.
9. **Dust with cocoa powder:**

- Before serving, dust the top of the tiramisu with unsweetened cocoa powder using a fine-mesh sieve.
10. **Serve and enjoy!** Slice and serve the tiramisu chilled. It's a perfect ending to a meal, especially with its rich coffee flavor and creamy texture.

Tiramisu is best enjoyed within a few days of making, as the ladyfinger biscuits continue to absorb moisture from the cream and coffee mixture. It's a delightful dessert that's sure to impress your guests!

Pineapple Upside-Down Cake

Ingredients:

For the topping:

- 1/4 cup unsalted butter
- 2/3 cup packed light brown sugar
- 7-8 pineapple slices (canned or fresh)
- Maraschino cherries, for garnish

For the cake batter:

- 1 1/2 cups all-purpose flour
- 1 1/2 teaspoons baking powder
- 1/2 teaspoon salt
- 1/2 cup unsalted butter, softened
- 1 cup granulated sugar
- 2 large eggs
- 1 teaspoon vanilla extract
- 1/2 cup milk

Instructions:

1. **Preheat** your oven to 350°F (175°C). Grease a 9-inch round cake pan or a 9x9-inch square baking pan.
2. **Prepare the topping:**
   - In a small saucepan, melt the butter over medium heat.
   - Add the brown sugar and stir until dissolved and bubbling, about 2-3 minutes.
   - Pour the mixture into the prepared cake pan, spreading it evenly.
3. **Arrange the pineapple and cherries:**
   - Arrange the pineapple slices over the brown sugar mixture in a single layer. You can cut the slices to fit as needed.
   - Place a maraschino cherry in the center of each pineapple slice and in any gaps between slices.
4. **Make the cake batter:**
   - In a medium bowl, whisk together the flour, baking powder, and salt.
5. **Cream butter and sugar:**
   - In a large bowl or the bowl of a stand mixer, beat the softened butter and granulated sugar together until light and fluffy.
6. **Add eggs and vanilla:**
   - Beat in the eggs, one at a time, until well combined.
   - Add the vanilla extract and mix until smooth.
7. **Combine wet and dry ingredients:**

- Gradually add the flour mixture to the butter mixture, alternating with the milk, beginning and ending with the flour mixture. Mix until just combined.

8. **Spread batter over topping:**
   - Carefully spread the cake batter over the pineapple and cherry layer in the cake pan, smoothing the top evenly.
9. **Bake the cake:**
   - Bake in the preheated oven for 40-45 minutes, or until a toothpick inserted into the center comes out clean and the top is golden brown.
10. **Cool and invert:**
    - Remove the cake from the oven and let it cool in the pan for about 10 minutes.
    - Place a serving plate upside-down over the top of the cake pan, then carefully invert the cake onto the plate. Slowly lift off the pan.
11. **Serve and enjoy!** Serve the pineapple upside-down cake warm or at room temperature. It's delicious on its own or with a dollop of whipped cream or a scoop of vanilla ice cream.

This homemade pineapple upside-down cake is a nostalgic dessert that's perfect for gatherings or any occasion. The combination of caramelized pineapple, cherries, and tender cake is sure to be a hit!

Almond Biscotti

Ingredients:

- 1 cup granulated sugar
- 1/2 cup unsalted butter, softened
- 3 large eggs
- 1 teaspoon almond extract
- 3 cups all-purpose flour
- 1 tablespoon baking powder
- 1/4 teaspoon salt
- 1 cup whole almonds, toasted and coarsely chopped (or slivered almonds)

Instructions:

1. **Preheat** your oven to 350°F (175°C). Line a baking sheet with parchment paper or a silicone baking mat.
2. **Cream butter and sugar:**
   - In a large bowl or the bowl of a stand mixer, beat together the softened butter and granulated sugar until light and fluffy.
3. **Add eggs and almond extract:**
   - Beat in the eggs, one at a time, until well combined.
   - Add the almond extract and mix until incorporated.
4. **Combine dry ingredients:**
   - In a separate bowl, whisk together the flour, baking powder, and salt.
5. **Mix dough:**
   - Gradually add the dry ingredients to the butter mixture, mixing until a dough forms.
   - Fold in the chopped almonds until evenly distributed.
6. **Shape the dough:**
   - Divide the dough in half. On a lightly floured surface, shape each half into a log about 12 inches long and 2 inches wide. Place the logs on the prepared baking sheet, spacing them apart.
7. **Bake the logs:**
   - Bake in the preheated oven for 25-30 minutes, or until the logs are firm to the touch and lightly golden brown.
8. **Cool slightly:**
   - Remove the baking sheet from the oven and let the logs cool on a wire rack for 10-15 minutes.
9. **Slice the biscotti:**
   - Using a sharp knife, carefully slice the logs diagonally into 1/2-inch thick slices.
10. **Bake again:**
    - Place the biscotti slices cut side down on the baking sheet. Return to the oven and bake for an additional 10-12 minutes, or until the biscotti are golden and crisp.

11. **Cool and store:**
    - Remove from the oven and let the biscotti cool completely on a wire rack.
    - Once cooled, store the almond biscotti in an airtight container at room temperature.
12. **Enjoy!** Serve almond biscotti with coffee, tea, or as a delightful snack. They also make lovely gifts when packaged in a decorative tin or box.

These homemade almond biscotti are crunchy, nutty, and perfect for dunking. They're a wonderful treat to enjoy any time of day!

Macarons

Ingredients:

For the macaron shells:

- 1 cup (100g) almond flour
- 1 3/4 cups (200g) powdered sugar
- 3 large egg whites, at room temperature
- 1/4 cup (50g) granulated sugar
- Gel food coloring (optional)

For the filling:

- 1/2 cup (115g) unsalted butter, softened
- 1 cup (120g) powdered sugar
- 1-2 tablespoons heavy cream
- 1 teaspoon vanilla extract (or flavoring of your choice)

Instructions:

1. **Prepare baking sheets:**
   - Line two baking sheets with parchment paper or silicone mats. You can also trace circles (about 1.5 inches in diameter) onto the parchment paper as a guide for piping.
2. **Make the almond mixture:**
   - In a food processor, combine the almond flour and powdered sugar. Pulse until finely ground and well combined. Sift the mixture into a large bowl to remove any lumps.
3. **Whip egg whites:**
   - In a clean, dry mixing bowl (preferably stainless steel or glass), beat the egg whites with an electric mixer on medium speed until foamy.
   - Gradually add the granulated sugar, a little at a time, while continuing to beat. Increase the speed to high and beat until stiff peaks form. The egg whites should be glossy and hold their shape.
4. **Macaronage (folding the mixture):**
   - Gently fold the almond flour mixture into the beaten egg whites using a spatula. Use about 10-15 gentle strokes to incorporate the dry ingredients. The batter should be smooth and flow like lava.
   - If desired, add gel food coloring at this stage and continue folding until evenly colored.
5. **Pipe the macarons:**
   - Transfer the batter to a piping bag fitted with a round tip (about 1/2 inch in diameter).

- Holding the piping bag vertically, pipe small rounds onto the prepared baking sheets, following the circles you traced earlier.
- Tap the baking sheets firmly against the counter to release any air bubbles. Let the piped macarons sit at room temperature for 30-60 minutes, until a skin forms on top. This helps create the characteristic "feet" of the macarons.

6. **Bake:**
   - Preheat your oven to 300°F (150°C) while the macarons are resting.
   - Bake the macarons, one sheet at a time, in the preheated oven for 15-18 minutes, rotating the sheet halfway through baking. The macarons should be set and firm, but not browned.

7. **Cool:**
   - Remove from the oven and let the macarons cool completely on the baking sheets before gently peeling them off the parchment paper.

8. **Make the filling:**
   - While the macarons are cooling, prepare the filling. In a mixing bowl, beat the softened butter until creamy.
   - Gradually add the powdered sugar, heavy cream, and vanilla extract. Beat until smooth and fluffy. Adjust consistency with more cream if needed.

9. **Assemble the macarons:**
   - Pair up the cooled macaron shells of similar size.
   - Pipe or spoon a small amount of filling onto the flat side of one shell. Gently press the flat side of another shell on top to sandwich them together.

10. **Mature the macarons (optional):**
    - Place the filled macarons in an airtight container and refrigerate for 24-48 hours. This helps the flavors meld and the texture to improve.

11. **Serve and enjoy!** Macarons are best enjoyed at room temperature. Store any leftovers in an airtight container in the refrigerator for up to 5 days.

Macarons require a bit of practice to perfect, especially mastering the consistency of the batter and baking time. Don't get discouraged if your first batch isn't perfect—they're still delicious even if they don't have perfect feet! Adjustments in technique and recipe can lead to beautiful, delicate macarons.

Chocolate Truffles

Ingredients:

- 8 oz (225g) good quality dark chocolate, finely chopped
- 1/2 cup (120ml) heavy cream
- 2 tablespoons unsalted butter, softened
- 1 teaspoon vanilla extract
- Cocoa powder, powdered sugar, chopped nuts, or melted chocolate, for coating

Instructions:

1. **Prepare the chocolate ganache:**
   - Place the chopped chocolate in a heatproof bowl.
   - In a small saucepan, heat the heavy cream over medium heat until it just begins to boil.
   - Pour the hot cream over the chopped chocolate and let it sit for 1-2 minutes.
   - Stir gently with a spatula until the chocolate is completely melted and smooth.
2. **Add butter and vanilla:**
   - Add the softened butter and vanilla extract to the chocolate ganache. Stir until the butter is melted and fully incorporated.
3. **Chill the ganache:**
   - Cover the bowl with plastic wrap, pressing the wrap directly onto the surface of the ganache to prevent a skin from forming.
   - Refrigerate the ganache for 2-3 hours, or until firm enough to scoop and roll into balls.
4. **Shape the truffles:**
   - Once chilled and firm, use a small spoon or a melon baller to scoop out portions of the ganache.
   - Roll each portion between your palms to form smooth balls. Work quickly to prevent the ganache from melting too much.
5. **Coat the truffles:**
   - Roll each truffle in cocoa powder, powdered sugar, chopped nuts, or dip them in melted chocolate for a glossy finish.
   - Place the coated truffles on a baking sheet lined with parchment paper.
6. **Chill and store:**
   - Refrigerate the truffles for about 30 minutes to firm up the coating.
7. **Serve and enjoy!** Chocolate truffles are best served at room temperature. Store any leftovers in an airtight container in the refrigerator for up to 2 weeks.

These homemade chocolate truffles are rich, smooth, and perfect for indulging yourself or gifting to loved ones. Experiment with different coatings and decorations to create a variety of flavors and textures!

Coconut Macaroons

Ingredients:

- 3 cups sweetened shredded coconut
- 2/3 cup sweetened condensed milk
- 2 large egg whites
- 1 teaspoon vanilla extract
- 1/4 teaspoon salt

Instructions:

1. **Preheat** your oven to 325°F (160°C). Line a baking sheet with parchment paper or a silicone baking mat.
2. **Mix ingredients:**
   - In a large bowl, combine the shredded coconut, sweetened condensed milk, vanilla extract, and salt. Mix well until evenly combined.
3. **Whip egg whites:**
   - In a separate bowl, beat the egg whites until stiff peaks form.
4. **Fold in egg whites:**
   - Gently fold the beaten egg whites into the coconut mixture until thoroughly combined. Be careful not to deflate the egg whites too much.
5. **Shape the macaroons:**
   - Using a spoon or a small cookie scoop, drop spoonfuls of the coconut mixture onto the prepared baking sheet, spacing them about 1 inch apart.
6. **Bake:**
   - Bake in the preheated oven for 20-25 minutes, or until the macaroons are lightly golden brown on the bottom and edges.
7. **Cool and store:**
   - Remove from the oven and let the macaroons cool on the baking sheet for a few minutes, then transfer them to a wire rack to cool completely.
8. **Optional drizzle (if desired):**
   - Melt some chocolate (dark, milk, or white) and drizzle it over the cooled macaroons for extra flavor and decoration.
9. **Serve and enjoy!** Coconut macaroons can be stored in an airtight container at room temperature for several days.

These coconut macaroons are naturally gluten-free and have a wonderful chewy texture with a hint of sweetness. They make a perfect treat for coconut lovers and are great for sharing on various occasions!

Cherry Cobbler

Ingredients:

For the cherry filling:

- 4 cups fresh or frozen cherries, pitted (about 2 lbs)
- 1/2 cup granulated sugar
- 1 tablespoon cornstarch
- 1/4 teaspoon almond extract (optional)
- 1 tablespoon lemon juice

For the cobbler topping:

- 1 cup all-purpose flour
- 1/4 cup granulated sugar
- 1 1/2 teaspoons baking powder
- 1/4 teaspoon salt
- 6 tablespoons unsalted butter, cold and cut into small pieces
- 1/3 cup milk

Instructions:

1. **Preheat** your oven to 375°F (190°C). Grease a 2-quart baking dish or a 9x9-inch square baking pan.
2. **Make the cherry filling:**
   - In a large bowl, combine the pitted cherries, granulated sugar, cornstarch, almond extract (if using), and lemon juice. Toss until the cherries are evenly coated.
3. **Transfer to baking dish:**
   - Pour the cherry mixture into the prepared baking dish, spreading it out evenly.
4. **Prepare the cobbler topping:**
   - In another bowl, whisk together the flour, granulated sugar, baking powder, and salt.
   - Cut in the cold butter pieces using a pastry cutter or your fingers, until the mixture resembles coarse crumbs.
5. **Add milk:**
   - Gradually add the milk to the flour mixture, stirring with a fork until just combined. The dough will be slightly sticky.
6. **Drop spoonfuls over cherries:**
   - Drop spoonfuls of the cobbler topping evenly over the cherry filling. It's okay if some of the cherries peek through.
7. **Bake the cobbler:**

- Place the baking dish on a baking sheet (to catch any spills) and bake in the preheated oven for 35-40 minutes, or until the topping is golden brown and the cherry filling is bubbly.

8. **Cool slightly:**
   - Remove from the oven and let the cherry cobbler cool for about 10-15 minutes before serving.
9. **Serve warm:**
   - Serve the cherry cobbler warm, optionally with a scoop of vanilla ice cream or whipped cream.
10. **Enjoy!** This homemade cherry cobbler is best enjoyed fresh from the oven, with its juicy cherry filling and tender, buttery topping. It's a comforting dessert that's perfect for sharing with friends and family!

Pumpkin Pie

Ingredients:

For the pie crust:

- 1 1/4 cups all-purpose flour
- 1/2 teaspoon salt
- 1/2 teaspoon granulated sugar
- 1/2 cup (1 stick) unsalted butter, cold and cut into small pieces
- 3-4 tablespoons ice water

For the pumpkin pie filling:

- 1 can (15 ounces) pumpkin puree (not pumpkin pie filling)
- 3/4 cup packed light brown sugar
- 1 teaspoon ground cinnamon
- 1/2 teaspoon ground ginger
- 1/4 teaspoon ground nutmeg
- 1/4 teaspoon ground cloves
- 1/2 teaspoon salt
- 2 large eggs
- 1 cup evaporated milk (or half-and-half)

Instructions:

1. **Make the pie crust:**
    - In a large bowl, whisk together the flour, salt, and sugar.
    - Add the cold butter pieces and cut them into the flour mixture using a pastry cutter or your fingers, until the mixture resembles coarse crumbs.
    - Gradually add the ice water, 1 tablespoon at a time, mixing with a fork until the dough just begins to come together.
    - Shape the dough into a ball, flatten into a disk, wrap tightly in plastic wrap, and refrigerate for at least 1 hour.
2. **Prepare the pie crust:**
    - On a lightly floured surface, roll out the chilled dough into a circle about 12 inches in diameter.
    - Carefully transfer the dough to a 9-inch pie dish. Trim any excess dough from the edges and crimp as desired. Refrigerate the crust while preparing the filling.
3. **Preheat** your oven to 425°F (220°C).
4. **Make the pumpkin pie filling:**
    - In a large bowl, combine the pumpkin puree, brown sugar, cinnamon, ginger, nutmeg, cloves, and salt. Mix until well combined and smooth.
    - Add the eggs and beat lightly until incorporated.

- Gradually stir in the evaporated milk (or half-and-half) until smooth and well combined.
5. **Fill and bake the pie:**
    - Pour the pumpkin pie filling into the chilled pie crust smoothing the top with a spatula.
6. **Bake:**
    - Place the pie in the preheated oven and bake for 15 minutes.
7. **Reduce temperature and continue baking:**
    - Reduce the oven temperature to 350°F (175°C) and bake for an additional 40-50 minutes, or until the filling is set and a knife inserted near the center comes out clean.
8. **Cool and serve:**
    - Remove the pie from the oven and let it cool completely on a wire rack.
    - Refrigerate for at least 2 hours or overnight before serving to allow the filling to set.
9. **Serve and enjoy!** Pumpkin pie is delicious served chilled or at room temperature, topped with whipped cream if desired.

This homemade pumpkin pie is rich, creamy, and full of warm spices, making it a perfect dessert for Thanksgiving or any fall gathering.

Cannoli

Ingredients:

For the cannoli shells:

- 1 1/2 cups all-purpose flour, plus extra for dusting
- 2 tablespoons granulated sugar
- 1/4 teaspoon salt
- 2 tablespoons unsalted butter, softened
- 1/2 cup sweet Marsala wine (or white wine)
- 1 large egg, lightly beaten
- Vegetable oil, for frying

For the cannoli filling:

- 2 cups whole milk ricotta cheese, drained if necessary
- 3/4 cup powdered sugar, sifted
- 1/2 teaspoon vanilla extract
- 1/4 cup mini chocolate chips (optional)
- Powdered sugar, for dusting

Instructions:

1. **Make the cannoli shells:**
    - In a large bowl, whisk together the flour, granulated sugar, and salt.
    - Cut in the softened butter using a pastry cutter or your fingers until the mixture resembles coarse crumbs.
    - Gradually add the Marsala wine and beaten egg, mixing until the dough comes together.
    - Turn the dough out onto a lightly floured surface and knead until smooth and elastic, about 5 minutes.
    - Wrap the dough in plastic wrap and let it rest at room temperature for at least 30 minutes.
2. **Roll and cut the dough:**
    - Divide the rested dough into 4 equal pieces. Keep the remaining dough covered with a clean kitchen towel.
    - On a lightly floured surface, roll out one piece of dough very thinly, about 1/8 inch thick.
    - Using a 3 to 4-inch round cutter or glass, cut out circles of dough. Gather and re-roll the scraps as needed.
    - Repeat with the remaining dough pieces.
3. **Shape and fry the cannoli shells:**
    - Heat about 2 inches of vegetable oil in a deep, heavy-bottomed pot or fryer to 350°F (175°C).

- Wrap each dough circle around a cannoli tube (metal tubes specifically made for shaping cannoli shells) and seal the edges with a dab of beaten egg.
- Carefully place the wrapped tubes into the hot oil, a few at a time, and fry until golden brown and crisp, about 2-3 minutes.
- Using tongs, carefully remove the cannoli shells from the oil and transfer to a paper towel-lined tray to drain and cool.

4. **Make the cannoli filling:**
   - In a mixing bowl, combine the ricotta cheese, powdered sugar, and vanilla extract. Mix until smooth and creamy.
   - Fold in the mini chocolate chips, if using.

5. **Fill the cannoli shells:**
   - Once the cannoli shells are cool enough to handle but still warm, gently slide the shells off the tubes.
   - Using a piping bag fitted with a large plain tip (or a zip-top bag with a corner cut off), pipe the ricotta filling into each end of the cannoli shell, filling from both ends to evenly distribute the filling.

6. **Serve and enjoy!**
   - Dust the filled cannoli with powdered sugar.
   - Serve immediately for best texture and flavor.

Cannoli are best enjoyed fresh, as the shells can soften over time once filled. They are a delightful treat with a crisp shell and creamy filling, perfect for special occasions or as a sweet indulgence!

Maple Pecan Bars

Ingredients:

For the crust:

- 1 cup all-purpose flour
- 1/4 cup granulated sugar
- 1/2 cup unsalted butter, cold and cut into small pieces

For the filling:

- 1/2 cup unsalted butter
- 1/2 cup packed light brown sugar
- 1/2 cup pure maple syrup
- 2 tablespoons heavy cream
- 2 cups pecan halves or pieces, roughly chopped

Instructions:

1. **Preheat** your oven to 350°F (175°C). Grease or line a 9x9-inch baking pan with parchment paper, leaving an overhang for easy removal.
2. **Make the crust:**
    - In a medium bowl, combine the flour and granulated sugar.
    - Cut in the cold butter using a pastry cutter or your fingers until the mixture resembles coarse crumbs.
    - Press the mixture evenly into the bottom of the prepared baking pan.
3. **Bake the crust:**
    - Bake in the preheated oven for 15-18 minutes, or until the crust is lightly golden brown. Remove from the oven and set aside.
4. **Prepare the filling:**
    - In a medium saucepan, melt the butter over medium heat.
    - Stir in the brown sugar, maple syrup, and heavy cream.
    - Cook, stirring constantly, until the mixture comes to a boil.
    - Remove from heat and stir in the chopped pecans.
5. **Assemble and bake:**
    - Pour the pecan filling evenly over the baked crust.
    - Return the pan to the oven and bake for an additional 20-25 minutes, or until the filling is bubbling and slightly set.
6. **Cool and slice:**
    - Remove from the oven and let the maple pecan bars cool completely in the pan on a wire rack.
    - Once cooled, lift the bars out of the pan using the parchment paper overhang.
    - Cut into squares or bars using a sharp knife.
7. **Serve and enjoy!**

- Maple pecan bars can be served at room temperature or chilled.
- Store any leftovers in an airtight container at room temperature for up to 3 days.

These maple pecan bars are rich, nutty, and perfectly sweetened with the natural flavor of maple syrup. They make a wonderful dessert or snack, especially during the fall and holiday seasons!

Coffee Cake

Ingredients:

For the cake:

- 2 cups all-purpose flour
- 1 teaspoon baking powder
- 1 teaspoon baking soda
- 1/2 teaspoon salt
- 1/2 cup unsalted butter, softened
- 1 cup granulated sugar
- 2 large eggs
- 1 cup sour cream or Greek yogurt
- 1 teaspoon vanilla extract

For the streusel topping:

- 1/2 cup packed light brown sugar
- 1/2 cup all-purpose flour
- 1 teaspoon ground cinnamon
- 1/4 cup unsalted butter, melted
- 1/2 cup chopped nuts (optional, such as pecans or walnuts)

Instructions:

1. **Preheat** your oven to 350°F (175°C). Grease and flour a 9x9-inch baking pan or line it with parchment paper for easy removal.
2. **Make the streusel topping:**
    - In a small bowl, combine the brown sugar, flour, cinnamon, melted butter, and chopped nuts (if using). Mix until crumbly and set aside.
3. **Prepare the cake batter:**
    - In a medium bowl, whisk together the flour, baking powder, baking soda, and salt.
    - In a separate large bowl, cream together the softened butter and granulated sugar until light and fluffy.
    - Beat in the eggs, one at a time, until well combined. Stir in the sour cream (or Greek yogurt) and vanilla extract until smooth.
4. **Combine the batter:**
    - Gradually add the dry ingredients to the wet ingredients, mixing until just combined. Be careful not to overmix.
5. **Assemble the coffee cake:**
    - Spread half of the batter into the prepared baking pan, smoothing it out evenly with a spatula.
    - Sprinkle half of the streusel topping evenly over the batter.

- - Carefully spread the remaining batter over the streusel layer, smoothing it out again.
  - Top with the remaining streusel mixture, covering the entire surface.
6. **Bake the coffee cake:**
   - Bake in the preheated oven for 35-40 minutes, or until a toothpick inserted into the center comes out clean or with a few moist crumbs.
7. **Cool and serve:**
   - Remove from the oven and let the coffee cake cool in the pan on a wire rack for at least 15 minutes.
   - Slice and serve warm or at room temperature. Enjoy with your favorite hot beverage!

This coffee cake recipe yields a moist and flavorful cake with a delightful crunchy streusel topping. It's perfect for breakfast, brunch, or as a comforting treat any time of the day!

S'mores Brownies

Ingredients:

For the brownie base:

- 1/2 cup (1 stick) unsalted butter
- 1 cup granulated sugar
- 2 large eggs
- 1 teaspoon vanilla extract
- 1/3 cup unsweetened cocoa powder
- 1/2 cup all-purpose flour
- 1/4 teaspoon salt
- 1/4 teaspoon baking powder

For the s'mores topping:

- 1 1/2 cups mini marshmallows
- 1/2 cup milk chocolate chips
- 1 cup crushed graham crackers (about 4-5 graham cracker sheets)

Instructions:

1. **Preheat** your oven to 350°F (175°C). Grease or line an 8x8-inch baking pan with parchment paper.
2. **Make the brownie base:**
   - In a medium saucepan, melt the butter over medium heat. Remove from heat and stir in the granulated sugar until well combined.
   - Add the eggs, one at a time, stirring well after each addition. Stir in the vanilla extract.
   - Add the cocoa powder, flour, salt, and baking powder to the saucepan. Stir until the batter is smooth and well combined.
3. **Bake the brownies:**
   - Pour the brownie batter into the prepared baking pan, spreading it out evenly with a spatula.
   - Bake in the preheated oven for 20-25 minutes, or until a toothpick inserted into the center comes out with a few moist crumbs.
4. **Add the s'mores topping:**
   - Remove the brownies from the oven and immediately sprinkle the mini marshmallows evenly over the top.
   - Scatter the milk chocolate chips and crushed graham crackers over the marshmallows.
5. **Broil the s'mores brownies:**
   - Preheat your oven's broiler.

- Place the pan of brownies under the broiler for 1-2 minutes, or until the marshmallows are toasted and golden brown. Watch carefully to prevent burning.

6. **Cool and serve:**
    - Remove from the oven and let the s'mores brownies cool in the pan on a wire rack.
    - Once cooled, lift the brownies out of the pan using the parchment paper overhang. Cut into squares and serve.

7. **Enjoy!**
    - These s'mores brownies are best enjoyed fresh, with the gooey marshmallows, melted chocolate, and crunchy graham crackers reminiscent of campfire s'mores. They are perfect for indulging in a nostalgic treat at home!

Lemon Meringue Pie

Ingredients:

For the pie crust:

- 1 1/4 cups all-purpose flour
- 1/2 teaspoon salt
- 1/2 cup unsalted butter, chilled and cut into small pieces
- 1/4 cup ice water

For the lemon filling:

- 1 cup granulated sugar
- 1/4 cup cornstarch
- 1/4 teaspoon salt
- 1 1/2 cups water
- 1/2 cup freshly squeezed lemon juice
- 3 large egg yolks
- 2 tablespoons unsalted butter
- 1 tablespoon finely grated lemon zest

For the meringue topping:

- 3 large egg whites, at room temperature
- 1/4 teaspoon cream of tartar
- 6 tablespoons granulated sugar
- 1/2 teaspoon vanilla extract

Instructions:

1. **Make the pie crust:**
   - In a food processor, pulse the flour and salt together.
   - Add the chilled butter pieces and pulse until the mixture resembles coarse crumbs.
   - Gradually add the ice water, 1 tablespoon at a time, pulsing until the dough comes together.
   - Shape the dough into a disk, wrap tightly in plastic wrap, and refrigerate for at least 1 hour.
2. **Preheat** your oven to 375°F (190°C). On a lightly floured surface, roll out the chilled dough into a circle about 12 inches in diameter. Transfer the dough to a 9-inch pie dish, trim any excess, and crimp the edges decoratively. Prick the bottom of the crust with a fork.
3. **Blind bake the pie crust:**
   - Line the pie crust with parchment paper or aluminum foil and fill with pie weights or dried beans.

- Bake for 15 minutes. Remove the parchment paper and weights, then bake for an additional 10-12 minutes, or until the crust is golden brown. Remove from the oven and set aside to cool.

4. **Make the lemon filling:**
   - In a medium saucepan, whisk together the sugar, cornstarch, and salt.
   - Gradually whisk in the water and lemon juice until smooth.
   - Cook over medium heat, stirring constantly, until the mixture thickens and comes to a boil.
   - Remove from heat. In a small bowl, whisk the egg yolks. Gradually whisk in about 1/2 cup of the hot lemon mixture to temper the yolks.
   - Gradually whisk the tempered egg yolk mixture back into the saucepan with the remaining hot lemon mixture.
   - Return to medium heat and cook, stirring constantly, for 2 minutes or until thickened.
   - Remove from heat and stir in the butter and lemon zest until smooth.

5. **Make the meringue topping:**
   - In a clean mixing bowl, beat the egg whites and cream of tartar on medium speed until soft peaks form.
   - Gradually add the granulated sugar, 1 tablespoon at a time, while beating on high speed until stiff peaks form.
   - Beat in the vanilla extract until well combined.

6. **Assemble the pie:**
   - Pour the hot lemon filling into the cooled pie crust spreading it out evenly.
   - Immediately spread the meringue topping over the hot lemon filling, starting at the edges to seal to the crust. Ensure the meringue touches the crust all around to prevent shrinking.

7. **Bake the pie:**
   - Bake in the preheated oven for 10-12 minutes, or until the meringue is golden brown.

8. **Cool and serve:**
   - Remove from the oven and cool the lemon meringue pie on a wire rack for at least 1 hour before slicing and serving.

9. **Enjoy!**
   - Serve the lemon meringue pie at room temperature or chilled. Store any leftovers in the refrigerator.

This lemon meringue pie is a delightful combination of tangy lemon filling and fluffy meringue topping, perfect for any occasion or as a refreshing dessert after a meal.

Gingerbread Cookies

Ingredients:

- 3 cups all-purpose flour
- 1 teaspoon baking powder
- 1/2 teaspoon baking soda
- 1/4 teaspoon salt
- 1 tablespoon ground ginger
- 1 1/2 teaspoons ground cinnamon
- 1/2 teaspoon ground cloves
- 1/2 cup unsalted butter, softened
- 1/2 cup packed brown sugar
- 1 large egg
- 1/2 cup molasses
- 1 teaspoon vanilla extract

For decorating:

- Royal icing (optional)
- Sprinkles, candies, or icing pens (optional)

Instructions:

1. **Prepare the dough:**
   - In a medium bowl, whisk together the flour, baking powder, baking soda, salt, ginger, cinnamon, and cloves. Set aside.
   - In a large mixing bowl, beat the softened butter and brown sugar together until creamy and smooth.
   - Add the egg, molasses, and vanilla extract to the butter-sugar mixture. Beat until well combined.
   - Gradually add the dry ingredients to the wet ingredients, mixing until the dough comes together. The dough should be firm but not sticky. If it's too sticky, add a little more flour.
2. **Chill the dough:**
   - Divide the dough into two equal portions. Flatten each portion into a disk, wrap tightly in plastic wrap, and refrigerate for at least 1 hour (or up to overnight).
3. **Preheat** your oven to 350°F (175°C). Line baking sheets with parchment paper.
4. **Roll out the dough:**
   - On a lightly floured surface, roll out one portion of the chilled dough to about 1/4 inch thickness. Use additional flour as needed to prevent sticking.
   - Use gingerbread cookie cutters to cut out shapes from the dough. Place the cut-out cookies onto the prepared baking sheets, spacing them about 1 inch apart.
5. **Bake the cookies:**

- Bake in the preheated oven for 8-10 minutes, or until the edges are firm and just beginning to brown. Avoid over-baking to keep the cookies chewy.
6. **Cool the cookies:**
    - Remove the cookies from the oven and let them cool on the baking sheets for a few minutes. Transfer to a wire rack to cool completely.
7. **Decorate (optional):**
    - Once the cookies are completely cool, you can decorate them with royal icing, sprinkles, candies, or icing pens. Let the icing set before storing or serving.
8. **Store:**
    - Store the gingerbread cookies in an airtight container at room temperature. They can be stored for up to 1 week.

Enjoy these homemade gingerbread cookies with a warm drink during the holiday season, or give them as gifts wrapped in festive packaging. They are a wonderful tradition and perfect for bringing a bit of spice and sweetness to any occasion!

Peach Crisp

Ingredients:

For the peach filling:

- 6 cups sliced fresh peaches (about 6-8 medium peaches)
- 1/4 cup granulated sugar (adjust based on the sweetness of the peaches)
- 1 tablespoon all-purpose flour
- 1 tablespoon lemon juice
- 1/2 teaspoon ground cinnamon
- 1/4 teaspoon ground nutmeg
- 1/4 teaspoon salt

For the oat topping:

- 1 cup old-fashioned rolled oats
- 1/2 cup all-purpose flour
- 1/2 cup packed light brown sugar
- 1/2 teaspoon ground cinnamon
- 1/4 teaspoon salt
- 1/2 cup unsalted butter, cold and cut into small pieces

Instructions:

1. **Preheat** your oven to 350°F (175°C). Grease a 9x9-inch baking dish or a similar-sized baking dish.
2. **Prepare the peach filling:**
    - In a large bowl, combine the sliced peaches, granulated sugar, flour, lemon juice, cinnamon, nutmeg, and salt. Toss gently until the peaches are evenly coated.
    - Transfer the peach mixture to the prepared baking dish, spreading it out evenly.
3. **Make the oat topping:**
    - In another bowl, combine the rolled oats, flour, brown sugar, cinnamon, and salt.
    - Add the cold butter pieces and use a pastry cutter or your fingers to mix until the mixture resembles coarse crumbs and the butter is well incorporated.
4. **Assemble and bake the peach crisp:**
    - Sprinkle the oat topping evenly over the peach filling in the baking dish.
    - Place the baking dish on a baking sheet (to catch any drips) and bake in the preheated oven for 40-45 minutes, or until the peach filling is bubbling and the topping is golden brown.
5. **Cool and serve:**
    - Remove from the oven and let the peach crisp cool for at least 10-15 minutes before serving.
    - Serve warm, optionally topped with vanilla ice cream or whipped cream.
6. **Enjoy!**

- Peach crisp is best enjoyed fresh and warm from the oven. The combination of tender peaches with the crunchy oat topping makes for a comforting and delicious dessert, perfect for any occasion.

This peach crisp recipe can be easily doubled for a larger crowd or adjusted based on personal preference. It's a wonderful way to celebrate ripe summer peaches or enjoy a taste of summer year-round!

Snickerdoodles

Ingredients:

For the cookie dough:

- 1 cup unsalted butter, softened
- 1 1/2 cups granulated sugar
- 2 large eggs
- 1 teaspoon vanilla extract
- 2 3/4 cups all-purpose flour
- 2 teaspoons cream of tartar
- 1 teaspoon baking soda
- 1/4 teaspoon salt

For rolling:

- 1/4 cup granulated sugar
- 1 tablespoon ground cinnamon

Instructions:

1. **Preheat** your oven to 375°F (190°C). Line baking sheets with parchment paper.
2. **Make the cookie dough:**
   - In a large bowl, cream together the softened butter and 1 1/2 cups of granulated sugar until light and fluffy.
   - Beat in the eggs one at a time, then stir in the vanilla extract.
   - In a separate bowl, whisk together the flour, cream of tartar, baking soda, and salt.
   - Gradually add the dry ingredients to the butter mixture, mixing until well combined.
3. **Roll the dough:**
   - In a small bowl, mix together 1/4 cup granulated sugar and ground cinnamon for rolling.
   - Shape the dough into 1-inch balls (about the size of a walnut) and roll each ball in the cinnamon-sugar mixture until coated.
4. **Bake the cookies:**
   - Place the coated dough balls onto the prepared baking sheets, spacing them about 2 inches apart.
   - Bake in the preheated oven for 8-10 minutes, or until the edges are set and just beginning to brown. The cookies will flatten slightly as they bake.
5. **Cool and enjoy:**
   - Remove from the oven and let the cookies cool on the baking sheets for a few minutes before transferring them to a wire rack to cool completely.

- Store the Snickerdoodles in an airtight container at room temperature. They can be stored for several days, but they are best enjoyed fresh.

Snickerdoodles are a delightful treat with their soft centers and crispy edges, coated in a cinnamon-sugar blend that adds a wonderful flavor. They are perfect for sharing with family and friends or enjoying with a glass of milk or hot beverage!

Black Forest Cake

Ingredients:

For the chocolate sponge cake:

- 1 3/4 cups all-purpose flour
- 3/4 cup unsweetened cocoa powder
- 2 cups granulated sugar
- 1 1/2 teaspoons baking powder
- 1 1/2 teaspoons baking soda
- 1 teaspoon salt
- 2 large eggs
- 1 cup whole milk
- 1/2 cup vegetable oil
- 2 teaspoons vanilla extract
- 1 cup boiling water

For the cherry filling:

- 1 can (21 ounces) cherry pie filling (or homemade cherry compote)
- 2 tablespoons cherry liqueur (optional)

For the whipped cream frosting:

- 3 cups heavy whipping cream, chilled
- 1/2 cup powdered sugar
- 1 teaspoon vanilla extract

For decoration (optional):

- Chocolate shavings or curls
- Maraschino cherries

Instructions:

1. **Prepare the chocolate sponge cake:**
    - Preheat your oven to 350°F (175°C). Grease and flour three 9-inch round cake pans.
    - In a large mixing bowl, sift together the flour, cocoa powder, granulated sugar, baking powder, baking soda, and salt.
    - Add the eggs, milk, oil, and vanilla extract. Beat on medium speed for 2 minutes.
    - Stir in the boiling water until the batter is well combined. The batter will be thin.
    - Divide the batter evenly among the prepared cake pans.
    - Bake in the preheated oven for 30-35 minutes, or until a toothpick inserted into the center comes out clean.

- Remove from the oven and let the cakes cool in the pans for 10 minutes before transferring them to wire racks to cool completely.
2. **Make the whipped cream frosting:**
    - In a large mixing bowl, beat the chilled heavy whipping cream, powdered sugar, and vanilla extract until stiff peaks form. Be careful not to overmix.
3. **Assemble the Black Forest Cake:**
    - Place one cooled chocolate cake layer on a serving plate or cake stand.
    - If using, brush the top of the cake layer with cherry liqueur for added flavor (optional).
    - Spread a layer of whipped cream frosting over the cake layer, followed by a layer of cherry pie filling or cherry compote.
    - Repeat with the second cake layer, frosting, and cherry filling.
    - Top with the third cake layer. Frost the top and sides of the cake with the remaining whipped cream frosting.
4. **Decorate the Black Forest Cake:**
    - Garnish the top of the cake with chocolate shavings or curls.
    - Pipe swirls of whipped cream frosting around the top edge of the cake.
    - Decorate with maraschino cherries or fresh cherries.
5. **Chill and serve:**
    - Refrigerate the Black Forest Cake for at least 1 hour before serving to allow the flavors to meld together and the whipped cream to set.
    - Slice and serve chilled. Enjoy this indulgent and classic Black Forest Cake!

This recipe captures the essence of a traditional Black Forest Cake with its rich chocolate layers, creamy whipped cream frosting, and tangy cherry filling. It's sure to impress at any special occasion or celebration!

Cranberry Orange Bread

Ingredients:

- 2 cups all-purpose flour
- 1 cup granulated sugar
- 1 1/2 teaspoons baking powder
- 1/2 teaspoon baking soda
- 1/2 teaspoon salt
- 3/4 cup freshly squeezed orange juice (about 2-3 oranges)
- 1/4 cup unsalted butter, melted and cooled
- 1 large egg, lightly beaten
- 1 tablespoon grated orange zest
- 1 1/2 cups fresh or frozen cranberries, coarsely chopped
- Optional: 1/2 cup chopped nuts (such as pecans or walnuts)

For the orange glaze (optional):

- 1 cup powdered sugar
- 2-3 tablespoons freshly squeezed orange juice

Instructions:

1. **Preheat** your oven to 350°F (175°C). Grease and flour a 9x5-inch loaf pan, or line it with parchment paper for easy removal.
2. **Prepare the batter:**
    - In a large bowl, whisk together the flour, sugar, baking powder, baking soda, and salt.
    - In a separate bowl, mix together the orange juice, melted butter, lightly beaten egg, and grated orange zest.
    - Pour the wet ingredients into the dry ingredients and stir until just combined. Do not overmix.
    - Gently fold in the chopped cranberries and nuts (if using) until evenly distributed in the batter.
3. **Bake the bread:**
    - Pour the batter into the prepared loaf pan and spread it out evenly.
    - Bake in the preheated oven for 55-65 minutes, or until a toothpick inserted into the center comes out clean.
4. **Cool the bread:**
    - Remove the bread from the oven and let it cool in the pan for 10-15 minutes.
    - Transfer the bread to a wire rack to cool completely.
5. **Make the orange glaze (optional):**
    - In a small bowl, whisk together the powdered sugar and 2-3 tablespoons of freshly squeezed orange juice until smooth and pourable.
6. **Glaze the bread (optional):**

- Once the bread has cooled completely, drizzle the orange glaze over the top.
7. **Slice and serve:**
    - Slice the cranberry orange bread and serve it at room temperature.
    - Enjoy this moist and flavorful bread as a breakfast treat, snack, or dessert!

This cranberry orange bread is perfect for sharing with family and friends, especially during the holiday season when cranberries and citrus are in abundance. It's a versatile recipe that can be enjoyed any time of year for its bright and refreshing flavors.

Eclairs

Ingredients:

For the choux pastry:

- 1/2 cup unsalted butter
- 1 cup water
- 1 cup all-purpose flour
- 1/4 teaspoon salt
- 4 large eggs, at room temperature

For the pastry cream:

- 2 cups whole milk
- 1/2 cup granulated sugar
- 4 large egg yolks
- 1/4 cup cornstarch
- 1 teaspoon vanilla extract

For the chocolate ganache:

- 1/2 cup heavy cream
- 4 ounces semi-sweet or dark chocolate, finely chopped

Instructions:

1. Make the choux pastry:

- Preheat your oven to 400°F (200°C). Line a baking sheet with parchment paper.
- In a medium saucepan, combine the butter and water. Bring to a boil over medium heat.
- Remove from heat and quickly stir in the flour and salt until the mixture forms a ball and pulls away from the sides of the pan.
- Transfer the mixture to a mixing bowl. Let it cool for about 5 minutes.
- Add the eggs one at a time, beating well after each addition, until the dough is smooth and glossy. The dough should be thick enough to pipe, but still able to hold its shape.
- Transfer the dough to a piping bag fitted with a large round tip (about 1/2-inch wide).
- Pipe the dough onto the prepared baking sheet into 4-inch lengths, spacing them about 2 inches apart.
- Bake in the preheated oven for 15 minutes, then reduce the oven temperature to 350°F (175°C) and bake for an additional 20-25 minutes, or until golden brown and puffed. Do not open the oven door during baking.
- Remove from the oven and let the eclairs cool completely on a wire rack.

2. Make the pastry cream:

- In a medium saucepan, heat the milk over medium heat until just simmering.
- In a separate bowl, whisk together the sugar, egg yolks, and cornstarch until smooth and pale.
- Gradually pour the hot milk into the egg mixture, whisking constantly.
- Return the mixture to the saucepan and cook over medium heat, stirring constantly, until thickened and it reaches a pudding-like consistency. This will take about 5-7 minutes.
- Remove from heat and stir in the vanilla extract.
- Transfer the pastry cream to a bowl and cover the surface with plastic wrap to prevent a skin from forming. Refrigerate until chilled.

3. Fill the eclairs:

- Once the eclairs and pastry cream are cooled, use a small piping tip or a knife to make 3 small holes on the bottom of each eclair.
- Fill a piping bag fitted with a small round tip with the chilled pastry cream. Pipe the cream into each eclair until filled.

4. Make the chocolate ganache:

- In a small saucepan, heat the heavy cream over medium heat until it just begins to simmer.
- Remove from heat and add the chopped chocolate. Let it sit for 1-2 minutes, then stir until smooth and glossy.

5. Glaze the eclairs:

- Dip the top of each filled eclair into the chocolate ganache or use a spoon to spread the ganache over the top.

6. Serve and enjoy:

- Place the glazed eclairs on a serving platter and refrigerate until the ganache is set.
- Serve chilled and enjoy these delicious homemade eclairs!

Eclairs are a labor of love but worth the effort for their delicate pastry and creamy filling. They make an impressive dessert for any occasion and are sure to delight anyone who tastes them!

Pistachio Baklava

Ingredients:

For the baklava:

- 1 package (16 ounces) phyllo dough, thawed if frozen
- 1 1/2 cups unsalted butter, melted
- 3 cups shelled pistachios, finely chopped
- 1 cup granulated sugar
- 1 teaspoon ground cinnamon
- 1/4 teaspoon ground cloves

For the syrup:

- 1 1/2 cups granulated sugar
- 1 cup water
- 1/2 cup honey
- 1 tablespoon lemon juice
- 1 cinnamon stick (optional)
- 1 teaspoon vanilla extract

Instructions:

1. **Prepare the syrup:**
   - In a medium saucepan, combine the sugar, water, honey, lemon juice, and cinnamon stick (if using). Bring to a boil over medium-high heat, stirring occasionally.
   - Reduce the heat to medium-low and simmer for 10-15 minutes, or until the syrup slightly thickens and reaches a thread-like consistency.
   - Remove from heat and stir in the vanilla extract. Let the syrup cool completely.
2. **Prepare the pistachio filling:**
   - In a bowl, combine the finely chopped pistachios, granulated sugar, ground cinnamon, and ground cloves. Mix well and set aside.
3. **Assemble the baklava:**
   - Preheat your oven to 350°F (175°C). Lightly grease a 9x13-inch baking dish.
   - Unroll the phyllo dough and cover it with a damp towel to prevent it from drying out.
   - Place one sheet of phyllo dough in the prepared baking dish and brush it generously with melted butter. Repeat with 7 more sheets of phyllo, brushing each layer with butter.
   - Sprinkle about 1/3 cup of the pistachio filling evenly over the buttered phyllo layers.

- Continue layering 8 sheets of phyllo dough, brushing each with butter and sprinkling with pistachio filling, until all the pistachio filling is used (reserve about 1/2 cup for topping).
- Finish with a final layer of 8 sheets of phyllo dough, brushing each with butter.

4. **Cut and bake the baklava:**
    - Using a sharp knife, carefully cut the baklava into diamond or square shapes, making sure to cut all the way through to the bottom.
    - Bake in the preheated oven for 45-50 minutes, or until the baklava is golden brown and crisp.
5. **Pour the syrup:**
    - Remove the baklava from the oven and immediately pour the cooled syrup evenly over the hot baklava, allowing it to seep into the cuts and layers.
6. **Cool and serve:**
    - Let the baklava cool completely in the baking dish, allowing it to absorb the syrup and set.
    - Serve the pistachio baklava at room temperature, garnished with any reserved pistachio filling if desired.
7. **Enjoy!**
    - Pistachio baklava is best enjoyed fresh, and it stores well in an airtight container at room temperature for several days.

This pistachio baklava recipe captures the essence of this classic Middle Eastern dessert, with its layers of crisp phyllo pastry, sweet pistachio filling, and aromatic syrup. It's perfect for special occasions or as a delightful treat with coffee or tea.

Peppermint Bark

Ingredients:

- 12 ounces semi-sweet or dark chocolate, chopped (or chocolate chips)
- 12 ounces white chocolate, chopped (or white chocolate chips)
- 1/2 teaspoon peppermint extract, divided
- 1/2 cup crushed candy canes or peppermint candies (about 6-8 candy canes)

Instructions:

1. **Prepare a baking sheet:**
   - Line a baking sheet with parchment paper or a silicone baking mat.
2. **Melt the semi-sweet/dark chocolate:**
   - In a microwave-safe bowl or using a double boiler, melt the semi-sweet or dark chocolate until smooth. If using a microwave, heat in 30-second intervals, stirring well after each interval.
   - Stir in 1/4 teaspoon of peppermint extract into the melted chocolate.
3. **Spread the dark chocolate:**
   - Pour the melted dark chocolate onto the prepared baking sheet. Use an offset spatula or the back of a spoon to spread it evenly into a thin layer, about 1/4 inch thick.
   - Tap the baking sheet gently on the counter to smooth out the chocolate.
   - Place the baking sheet in the refrigerator for about 15-20 minutes, or until the dark chocolate layer is firm.
4. **Melt the white chocolate:**
   - In a separate microwave-safe bowl or double boiler, melt the white chocolate until smooth.
   - Stir in the remaining 1/4 teaspoon of peppermint extract into the melted white chocolate.
5. **Add crushed peppermint candies:**
   - Remove the baking sheet from the refrigerator. Pour the melted white chocolate over the chilled dark chocolate layer.
   - Quickly spread the white chocolate evenly over the dark chocolate layer.
   - Immediately sprinkle the crushed peppermint candies evenly over the top of the white chocolate layer, pressing them down gently with your fingers or the back of a spoon.
6. **Chill and break into pieces:**
   - Return the baking sheet to the refrigerator and chill for about 30 minutes to 1 hour, or until the peppermint bark is completely firm.
   - Once firm, lift the parchment paper or silicone mat with the peppermint bark onto a cutting board.
   - Use a sharp knife or your hands to break the peppermint bark into pieces of your desired size and shape.
7. **Serve and store:**

- Arrange the peppermint bark pieces on a serving plate or in gift bags.
- Store the peppermint bark in an airtight container at room temperature or in the refrigerator for up to 2 weeks.

Peppermint bark makes a wonderful homemade gift during the holidays and is a delightful treat to enjoy with friends and family. It's simple to customize by adjusting the amount of peppermint extract or adding other toppings like chopped nuts or drizzled chocolate. Enjoy this festive and delicious treat!

Butterscotch Pudding

Ingredients:

- 1/2 cup packed dark brown sugar
- 2 tablespoons cornstarch
- 1/4 teaspoon salt
- 2 1/2 cups whole milk
- 2 large egg yolks
- 2 tablespoons unsalted butter
- 1 teaspoon vanilla extract

Instructions:

1. **Combine dry ingredients:**
   - In a medium saucepan, whisk together the dark brown sugar, cornstarch, and salt until well combined.
2. **Add milk:**
   - Gradually whisk in the whole milk until smooth.
3. **Cook the mixture:**
   - Place the saucepan over medium heat and cook the mixture, stirring constantly, until it thickens and comes to a boil. This will take about 5-7 minutes.
4. **Temper the egg yolks:**
   - In a small bowl, lightly beat the egg yolks.
   - Gradually whisk about 1/2 cup of the hot milk mixture into the egg yolks to temper them, whisking constantly to prevent curdling.
   - Pour the tempered egg yolks back into the saucepan with the remaining hot milk mixture, whisking constantly.
5. **Simmer and thicken:**
   - Cook the pudding mixture over medium heat, stirring constantly, until it thickens further and coats the back of a spoon. This will take about 2-3 minutes.
6. **Add butter and vanilla:**
   - Remove the saucepan from the heat and stir in the unsalted butter and vanilla extract until the butter is melted and incorporated.
7. **Chill:**
   - Pour the butterscotch pudding into serving dishes or a large bowl.
   - Place a piece of plastic wrap directly on the surface of the pudding to prevent a skin from forming.
   - Refrigerate the pudding for at least 2 hours, or until chilled and set.
8. **Serve:**
   - Serve the butterscotch pudding chilled, optionally topped with whipped cream or a sprinkle of sea salt for extra flavor.
9. **Enjoy:**
   - Enjoy the creamy and caramelized flavors of homemade butterscotch pudding as a comforting dessert!

This butterscotch pudding recipe is perfect for those who enjoy a rich, caramel-like flavor in their desserts. It's simple to make from scratch and is sure to be a hit with family and friends!

Fig Newtons

Ingredients:

For the dough:

- 1 1/2 cups all-purpose flour
- 1/2 teaspoon baking powder
- 1/4 teaspoon salt
- 1/2 cup unsalted butter, softened
- 1/2 cup granulated sugar
- 1 large egg
- 1 teaspoon vanilla extract

For the fig filling:

- 1 1/2 cups dried figs, stems removed and roughly chopped
- 1/2 cup water
- 1/4 cup honey
- 1/2 teaspoon vanilla extract
- Zest of 1 lemon (optional)

Instructions:

1. **Prepare the fig filling:**
    - In a small saucepan, combine the dried figs and water. Bring to a simmer over medium heat.
    - Reduce the heat to low and simmer for 10-15 minutes, or until the figs are softened and the mixture is thickened.
    - Remove from heat and let cool slightly.
    - Transfer the fig mixture to a food processor or blender. Add honey, vanilla extract, and lemon zest (if using). Blend until smooth and well combined. Set aside to cool completely.
2. **Make the dough:**
    - In a medium bowl, whisk together the flour, baking powder, and salt.
    - In a separate large bowl, cream together the softened butter and granulated sugar until light and fluffy.
    - Beat in the egg and vanilla extract until well combined.
    - Gradually add the dry ingredients to the butter mixture, mixing until a soft dough forms.
3. **Assemble the Fig Newtons:**
    - Preheat your oven to 350°F (175°C). Line a baking sheet with parchment paper.
    - Divide the dough into two equal portions.
    - On a lightly floured surface, roll out one portion of the dough into a rectangle about 12x8 inches and 1/4 inch thick.

- Spread half of the fig filling evenly over the rolled-out dough, leaving a small border around the edges.
- Carefully fold one long side of the dough over the filling, then fold the other long side over to overlap and seal the filling inside. Press the seam lightly to seal.
- Gently transfer the filled dough log to the prepared baking sheet, seam side down.
- Repeat the process with the remaining dough and fig filling.

4. **Bake the Fig Newtons:**
   - Bake in the preheated oven for 20-25 minutes, or until the dough is golden brown and cooked through.
5. **Cool and slice:**
   - Remove from the oven and let cool on the baking sheet for 10 minutes.
   - Transfer the baked logs to a cutting board and slice diagonally into 1-inch wide pieces while still warm.
6. **Serve and store:**
   - Serve the Fig Newtons warm or at room temperature.
   - Store any leftovers in an airtight container at room temperature for up to 1 week.

Enjoy these homemade Fig Newtons as a delicious snack or dessert, with the natural sweetness of figs and the tender, buttery crust!

German Chocolate Cake

Ingredients:

For the chocolate cake:

- 2 cups all-purpose flour
- 1 cup unsweetened cocoa powder
- 1 1/2 teaspoons baking powder
- 1 1/2 teaspoons baking soda
- 1/2 teaspoon salt
- 2 cups granulated sugar
- 1 cup packed light brown sugar
- 4 large eggs, at room temperature
- 1 cup vegetable oil
- 1 cup buttermilk, at room temperature
- 2 teaspoons vanilla extract
- 1 cup boiling water

For the coconut-pecan frosting:

- 1 cup evaporated milk
- 1 cup granulated sugar
- 3 large egg yolks
- 1/2 cup unsalted butter
- 1 teaspoon vanilla extract
- 1 1/3 cups sweetened shredded coconut
- 1 cup chopped pecans

Instructions:

1. **Make the chocolate cake:**
   - Preheat your oven to 350°F (175°C). Grease and flour three 9-inch round cake pans.
   - In a large bowl, sift together the flour, cocoa powder, baking powder, baking soda, and salt.
   - In another bowl, beat the granulated sugar, brown sugar, and eggs until light and fluffy.
   - Add the vegetable oil, buttermilk, and vanilla extract to the egg mixture. Beat until well combined.
   - Gradually add the dry ingredients to the wet ingredients, mixing on low speed until just incorporated.
   - Stir in the boiling water, mixing until the batter is smooth. The batter will be thin.
   - Divide the batter evenly among the prepared cake pans.

- Bake in the preheated oven for 30-35 minutes, or until a toothpick inserted into the center of the cakes comes out clean.
- Remove from the oven and let the cakes cool in the pans for 10 minutes before transferring them to wire racks to cool completely.

2. **Make the coconut-pecan frosting:**
   - In a medium saucepan, whisk together the evaporated milk, granulated sugar, egg yolks, and butter.
   - Cook over medium heat, stirring constantly, until the mixture thickens and begins to bubble. This will take about 10-12 minutes.
   - Remove from heat and stir in the vanilla extract, shredded coconut, and chopped pecans.
   - Let the frosting cool to room temperature, stirring occasionally to help it thicken.

3. **Assemble the German Chocolate Cake:**
   - Place one cooled cake layer on a serving plate or cake stand.
   - Spread a generous layer of the coconut-pecan frosting over the top of the cake layer.
   - Repeat with the second and third cake layers, spreading frosting between each layer and on top.

4. **Decorate (optional):**
   - Use any remaining frosting to decorate the sides of the cake if desired.

5. **Chill and serve:**
   - Refrigerate the cake for at least 1 hour before serving to allow the frosting to set.
   - Slice and serve the German Chocolate Cake at room temperature. Enjoy this decadent and classic dessert!

This recipe yields a moist chocolate cake with a wonderfully nutty and coconutty frosting that complements the rich chocolate layers perfectly. It's sure to be a hit at any celebration or special occasion!

Rice Krispies Treats

Ingredients:

- 6 cups crispy rice cereal (such as Rice Krispies)
- 10 ounces (about 4 cups) marshmallows
- 3 tablespoons unsalted butter
- 1/2 teaspoon vanilla extract (optional)
- Pinch of salt (optional)

Instructions:

1. **Prepare the pan:**
   - Grease a 9x13-inch baking pan or line it with parchment paper. Set aside.
2. **Melt the marshmallows and butter:**
   - In a large saucepan, melt the butter over low heat.
   - Add the marshmallows to the melted butter, stirring constantly until completely melted and smooth. If using vanilla extract and salt, add them now and stir until combined.
3. **Mix in the cereal:**
   - Remove the saucepan from the heat.
   - Add the crispy rice cereal to the marshmallow mixture. Use a spatula or wooden spoon to gently fold and stir until the cereal is evenly coated with the marshmallow mixture.
4. **Press into the pan:**
   - Transfer the mixture to the prepared baking pan.
   - Use a greased spatula or your hands (lightly greased or dampened with water) to press the mixture evenly into the pan. Press firmly to compact the cereal treats.
5. **Cool and cut:**
   - Let the Rice Krispies Treats cool at room temperature for about 30 minutes, or until firm and set.
   - Use a sharp knife to cut into squares or rectangles of your desired size.
6. **Serve:**
   - Serve the Rice Krispies Treats at room temperature.
   - Store any leftovers in an airtight container at room temperature for up to 3 days. For longer storage, place them in the refrigerator for up to 1 week.

Variations:

- **Chocolate Drizzle:** Melt chocolate chips and drizzle over the cooled treats before cutting.
- **Peanut Butter:** Stir in 1/2 cup of creamy peanut butter with the marshmallows and butter mixture.
- **Fruity Pebbles:** Substitute crispy rice cereal with Fruity Pebbles cereal for a colorful twist.

Rice Krispies Treats are quick to make and always a crowd-pleaser, perfect for parties, snacks, or a sweet treat any time of day!

Mocha Ice Cream

Ingredients:

- 1 cup whole milk
- 1 cup heavy cream
- 3/4 cup granulated sugar
- 1/4 cup unsweetened cocoa powder
- 2 tablespoons instant espresso powder or instant coffee granules
- 4 large egg yolks
- 1 teaspoon vanilla extract
- 1/2 cup chocolate chips or chopped chocolate (optional, for extra richness)

Instructions:

1. **Prepare the ice cream base:**
    - In a medium saucepan, whisk together the whole milk, heavy cream, granulated sugar, cocoa powder, and instant espresso powder (or instant coffee granules).
    - Heat the mixture over medium heat, stirring frequently, until it begins to simmer. Remove from heat.
2. **Temper the egg yolks:**
    - In a separate bowl, whisk the egg yolks until smooth.
    - Gradually pour about 1/2 cup of the hot milk mixture into the egg yolks, whisking constantly to temper the yolks and prevent them from curdling.
    - Pour the tempered egg yolk mixture back into the saucepan with the remaining hot milk mixture, whisking constantly.
3. **Cook the custard:**
    - Cook the custard mixture over medium heat, stirring constantly with a wooden spoon or heatproof spatula, until it thickens enough to coat the back of the spoon. This will take about 5-7 minutes. Do not let it boil.
    - The custard is ready when you can draw a line with your finger on the back of the spoon and the line holds its shape.
4. **Strain the custard (optional):**
    - For a smoother texture, strain the custard through a fine-mesh sieve into a clean bowl to remove any lumps or bits of cooked egg.
5. **Cool the custard:**
    - Stir in the vanilla extract and optional chocolate chips or chopped chocolate (if using) until melted and smooth.
    - Cover the bowl with plastic wrap, pressing it directly onto the surface of the custard to prevent a skin from forming.
    - Refrigerate the custard until completely chilled, at least 4 hours or overnight.
6. **Churn the ice cream:**
    - Once chilled, pour the custard into an ice cream maker and churn according to the manufacturer's instructions until it reaches a soft-serve consistency.
7. **Freeze the ice cream:**

- Transfer the churned ice cream to a freezer-safe container.
- Press a piece of parchment paper or plastic wrap onto the surface of the ice cream to prevent ice crystals from forming.
- Freeze for at least 4 hours, or until firm.

8. **Serve and enjoy:**
   - Scoop the mocha ice cream into bowls or cones.
   - Garnish with chocolate shavings, cocoa powder, or whipped cream if desired.
   - Enjoy the creamy and flavorful mocha ice cream as a refreshing dessert or treat

Homemade mocha ice cream is a delightful way to enjoy the combination of coffee and chocolate flavors in a cool and creamy dessert. Adjust the sweetness and intensity of coffee to suit your taste preferences for a perfect batch every time!

Raspberry Sorbet

Ingredients:

- 4 cups fresh or frozen raspberries
- 1 cup granulated sugar
- 1 cup water
- 2 tablespoons fresh lemon juice
- 1-2 tablespoons vodka or raspberry liqueur (optional, helps with texture)

Instructions:

1. **Prepare the raspberries:**
   - If using fresh raspberries, rinse them under cold water and remove any stems or leaves. If using frozen raspberries, thaw them slightly.
2. **Make the simple syrup:**
   - In a small saucepan, combine the granulated sugar and water. Heat over medium-high heat, stirring occasionally, until the sugar completely dissolves and the mixture comes to a boil.
   - Remove the saucepan from heat and let the simple syrup cool to room temperature.
3. **Blend the raspberries:**
   - In a blender or food processor, puree the raspberries until smooth.
4. **Strain (optional):**
   - For a smoother sorbet, strain the raspberry puree through a fine-mesh sieve to remove the seeds. Use a spatula or spoon to press the puree through the sieve, leaving the seeds behind.
5. **Mix the sorbet base:**
   - In a large bowl, combine the raspberry puree, cooled simple syrup, fresh lemon juice, and vodka or raspberry liqueur (if using). Stir until well combined.
6. **Chill the mixture:**
   - Cover the bowl with plastic wrap and refrigerate the raspberry sorbet mixture for at least 2 hours, or until thoroughly chilled.
7. **Churn the sorbet:**
   - Once chilled, pour the raspberry sorbet mixture into an ice cream maker and churn according to the manufacturer's instructions until it reaches a soft-serve consistency.
8. **Freeze the sorbet:**
   - Transfer the churned sorbet into a freezer-safe container.
   - Press a piece of parchment paper or plastic wrap onto the surface of the sorbet to prevent ice crystals from forming.
   - Freeze for at least 4 hours, or until firm.
9. **Serve and enjoy:**
   - Scoop the raspberry sorbet into bowls or cones.

- Garnish with fresh raspberries, mint leaves, or a sprinkle of powdered sugar if desired.
- Enjoy the refreshing and fruity raspberry sorbet as a delightful dessert or palate cleanser!

Homemade raspberry sorbet is a light and flavorful treat that captures the natural sweetness and tartness of raspberries. It's perfect for serving after a meal or as a cool snack on a warm day. Adjust the sweetness and tartness by tasting the raspberry mixture before freezing to suit your preferences.

Orange Creamsicles

Ingredients:

- 1 cup fresh orange juice (about 4-5 oranges)
- Zest of 1 orange (optional, for extra flavor)
- 1 cup heavy cream
- 1/2 cup granulated sugar
- 1 teaspoon vanilla extract

Instructions:

1. **Prepare the orange mixture:**
   - In a bowl, combine the fresh orange juice and optional orange zest. Stir well and set aside.
2. **Make the cream mixture:**
   - In another bowl, whisk together the heavy cream, granulated sugar, and vanilla extract until the sugar is dissolved and the mixture is smooth.
3. **Combine the mixtures:**
   - Gradually pour the cream mixture into the orange juice mixture, stirring gently to combine. Be careful not to overmix to avoid excessive air bubbles.
4. **Pour into molds:**
   - Pour the combined mixture into popsicle molds. Leave a little space at the top to allow for expansion during freezing.
5. **Insert sticks:**
   - Place sticks or popsicle handles into each mold. If your molds don't have sticks, you can insert wooden sticks into the center of each filled mold.
6. **Freeze:**
   - Freeze the Orange Creamsicles for at least 4-6 hours, or until completely frozen.
7. **Unmold and serve:**
   - To unmold, run warm water over the outside of the molds for a few seconds to loosen the creamsicles.
   - Gently pull on the sticks to remove the creamsicles from the molds.
8. **Enjoy:**
   - Serve and enjoy these homemade Orange Creamsicles immediately.
   - Store any leftovers in the freezer in an airtight container or wrapped individually in plastic wrap.

These homemade Orange Creamsicles are creamy, refreshing, and bursting with citrus flavor. They make a perfect treat for hot summer days or anytime you crave a cool, fruity dessert. Feel free to adjust the sweetness by adding more or less sugar to suit your taste preferences.

Churros

Ingredients:

- 1 cup water
- 2 tablespoons white sugar
- 1/2 teaspoon salt
- 2 tablespoons vegetable oil
- 1 cup all-purpose flour
- Vegetable oil, for frying
- 1/4 cup white sugar, for coating
- 1/2 teaspoon ground cinnamon (optional, for coating)

Instructions:

1. **Prepare the churro dough:**
    - In a small saucepan over medium heat, combine water, 2 tablespoons of sugar, salt, and 2 tablespoons of vegetable oil. Bring to a boil and remove from heat.
    - Stir in flour until the mixture forms a ball. It should come together into a smooth dough.
2. **Fry the churros:**
    - Heat vegetable oil for frying in a deep-fryer or large pot to 375°F (190°C). You can test if the oil is ready by dropping a small piece of dough in; it should sizzle and float to the surface.
    - Transfer the dough to a pastry bag fitted with a large star tip.
    - Pipe 4-6 inch strips of dough into the hot oil, cutting them with scissors. You can fry 3-4 churros at a time, depending on the size of your pot.
    - Fry until golden brown, about 2-3 minutes on each side. Drain on paper towels.
3. **Coat the churros:**
    - Mix together 1/4 cup of sugar and cinnamon (if using) in a shallow dish.
    - Roll the hot churros in the cinnamon sugar mixture until evenly coated.
4. **Serve:**
    - Serve churros warm, optionally with chocolate sauce, caramel sauce, or dulce de leche for dipping.
5. **Enjoy:**
    - Enjoy these homemade churros as a delightful treat with friends and family!

Churros are best enjoyed fresh and warm, but you can store any leftovers in an airtight container at room temperature for a day. Reheat briefly in the oven or toaster oven to enjoy them again crispy.

Panna Cotta

Ingredients:

- 2 cups heavy cream
- 1/2 cup granulated sugar
- 1 teaspoon vanilla extract
- 1 packet (about 2 1/4 teaspoons) of powdered gelatin
- 1/4 cup cold water

Instructions:

1. **Prepare the gelatin:**
   - In a small bowl, sprinkle the gelatin over the cold water. Let it sit for about 5-10 minutes to soften.
2. **Heat the cream mixture:**
   - In a saucepan, combine the heavy cream and granulated sugar. Heat over medium heat, stirring occasionally, until the sugar has dissolved and the mixture is just about to simmer (do not boil).
   - Remove the saucepan from the heat and stir in the vanilla extract.
3. **Dissolve the gelatin:**
   - Microwave the bowl of gelatin and water for about 10-15 seconds, or until the gelatin is completely dissolved and becomes liquid.
   - Alternatively, you can place the bowl of gelatin over a small pot of simmering water and stir until dissolved.
4. **Combine the mixtures:**
   - Gradually whisk the dissolved gelatin into the warm cream mixture until completely incorporated.
5. **Pour into molds:**
   - Lightly grease or spray molds with cooking spray if not using silicone molds.
   - Divide the mixture evenly among your molds or ramekins. Tap gently on the counter to remove air bubbles.
6. **Chill:**
   - Cover the molds with plastic wrap or foil and refrigerate for at least 4 hours, or until the panna cotta is set and firm.
7. **Serve:**
   - To serve, gently run a knife around the edge of each mold and invert onto a serving plate.
   - Serve panna cotta chilled, garnished with fresh berries, fruit coulis, or a drizzle of honey.
8. **Enjoy:**
   - Enjoy the creamy and silky texture of homemade panna cotta as a delightful dessert!

Panna cotta can be prepared ahead of time and stored in the refrigerator for up to 2-3 days. It's a versatile dessert that can be flavored with various extracts (like almond or citrus) or served with different toppings to suit your taste preferences.

Marble Pound Cake

Ingredients:

- 1 cup (2 sticks) unsalted butter, softened
- 1 ½ cups granulated sugar
- 4 large eggs, at room temperature
- 1 teaspoon vanilla extract
- 2 cups all-purpose flour
- 1 teaspoon baking powder
- 1/4 teaspoon salt
- 1/2 cup milk
- 1/4 cup unsweetened cocoa powder

Instructions:

1. Preheat your oven to 350°F (175°C). Grease and flour a 9x5-inch loaf pan or line it with parchment paper.
2. In a large bowl, cream together the softened butter and granulated sugar until light and fluffy using a hand mixer or stand mixer.
3. Add the eggs, one at a time, beating well after each addition. Mix in the vanilla extract.
4. In a separate bowl, whisk together the all-purpose flour, baking powder, and salt.
5. Gradually add the dry ingredients to the butter mixture, alternating with the milk, beginning and ending with the flour mixture. Mix until just combined.
6. Transfer half of the batter to a separate bowl.
7. In a small bowl, mix the unsweetened cocoa powder with 2 tablespoons of hot water to create a smooth chocolate paste.
8. Fold the cocoa paste into one half of the batter until fully combined. This will be your chocolate batter.
9. To create the marbled effect, spoon dollops of the vanilla batter and chocolate batter alternately into the prepared loaf pan. Use a knife or skewer to gently swirl the batters together to create a marbled pattern.
10. Bake in the preheated oven for 50-60 minutes, or until a toothpick inserted into the center of the cake comes out clean.
11. Allow the marble pound cake to cool in the pan for 10-15 minutes before transferring it to a wire rack to cool completely.
12. Once cooled, slice and serve your marble pound cake. Enjoy the delicious combination of vanilla and chocolate flavors!

This marble pound cake is perfect for serving as a dessert or sweet treat with coffee or tea. It's moist, flavorful, and sure to be a hit with friends and family.

Bourbon Balls

Ingredients:

- 1 cup finely crushed vanilla wafer cookies (about 40 cookies)
- 1 cup finely chopped pecans
- 1 cup confectioners' sugar (powdered sugar), divided
- 2 tablespoons unsweetened cocoa powder
- 1/4 cup bourbon whiskey
- 2 tablespoons light corn syrup
- Additional confectioners' sugar for rolling

Instructions:

1. **Prepare the ingredients:**
   - In a large bowl, combine the finely crushed vanilla wafer cookies, chopped pecans, 1/2 cup of confectioners' sugar, and cocoa powder. Mix well.
2. **Add the wet ingredients:**
   - Stir in the bourbon whiskey and light corn syrup until the mixture is well combined and forms a dough-like consistency.
3. **Shape the bourbon balls:**
   - Using clean hands, scoop out about a tablespoon of the mixture and roll it into a ball between your palms.
   - Place the rolled bourbon ball onto a baking sheet lined with parchment paper or wax paper. Repeat until all of the mixture is used, making approximately 24 bourbon balls.
4. **Coat with confectioners' sugar:**
   - Roll each bourbon ball in the remaining 1/2 cup of confectioners' sugar until evenly coated. This gives them a nice powdered finish.
5. **Chill and serve:**
   - Place the bourbon balls in an airtight container and refrigerate for at least 1-2 hours, or until firm.
   - Serve chilled and enjoy these delicious bourbon balls as a decadent dessert or treat.

These bourbon balls can be stored in the refrigerator for up to 1 week, making them a perfect make-ahead dessert for parties or as gifts. The combination of bourbon, chocolate, and pecans creates a rich and indulgent flavor that's sure to be a hit with bourbon enthusiasts and dessert lovers alike!

Neapolitan Cupcakes

Ingredients:

- **For the Cupcakes:**
    - 1 1/2 cups all-purpose flour
    - 1 1/2 teaspoons baking powder
    - 1/4 teaspoon salt
    - 1/2 cup unsalted butter, softened
    - 1 cup granulated sugar
    - 2 large eggs, at room temperature
    - 1 teaspoon vanilla extract
    - 1/2 cup whole milk
- **For the Strawberry Frosting:**
    - 1/2 cup unsalted butter, softened
    - 2 cups confectioners' sugar (powdered sugar)
    - 1/2 cup fresh strawberries, pureed (about 6-8 strawberries)
    - 1/2 teaspoon vanilla extract
    - Pinch of salt
- **For the Chocolate Frosting:**
    - 1/2 cup unsalted butter, softened
    - 1 1/2 cups confectioners' sugar (powdered sugar)
    - 1/4 cup unsweetened cocoa powder
    - 1/2 teaspoon vanilla extract
    - 2-3 tablespoons whole milk or cream, as needed

Instructions:

1. **Make the Cupcakes:**
    - Preheat your oven to 350°F (175°C). Line a muffin tin with cupcake liners.
    - In a medium bowl, whisk together the flour, baking powder, and salt. Set aside.
    - In a large bowl, cream together the softened butter and granulated sugar until light and fluffy, using a hand mixer or stand mixer.
    - Add the eggs one at a time, beating well after each addition. Mix in the vanilla extract.
    - Gradually add the flour mixture to the butter mixture, alternating with the milk, beginning and ending with the flour mixture. Mix until just combined.
    - Divide the batter evenly into three bowls.
    - Leave one bowl as vanilla batter.
    - To one bowl, fold in 1/4 cup of strawberry puree until well combined, creating the strawberry batter.
    - To the last bowl, fold in 2 tablespoons of unsweetened cocoa powder and mix until combined, creating the chocolate batter.
    - Spoon a tablespoon of each batter (vanilla, strawberry, and chocolate) into each cupcake liner, filling each liner about 2/3 full.

- Bake for 18-20 minutes, or until a toothpick inserted into the center of a cupcake comes out clean.
- Remove from the oven and let cool in the muffin tin for 5 minutes before transferring to a wire rack to cool completely.

2. **Make the Frostings:**
    - **Strawberry Frosting:**
        - In a medium bowl, cream the softened butter until smooth.
        - Gradually add the confectioners' sugar, one cup at a time, mixing well after each addition.
        - Add the strawberry puree, vanilla extract, and a pinch of salt. Beat until smooth and fluffy. Adjust consistency with more powdered sugar or a splash of milk if needed. Set aside.
    - **Chocolate Frosting:**
        - In a separate bowl, cream the softened butter until smooth.
        - Gradually add the confectioners' sugar and cocoa powder, mixing well after each addition.
        - Add the vanilla extract and enough whole milk or cream, a tablespoon at a time, until the frosting is smooth and creamy.

3. **Assemble the Cupcakes:**
    - Once the cupcakes are completely cool, frost each cupcake with a swirl of strawberry frosting and chocolate frosting using a piping bag or spatula.
    - Optionally, garnish with chocolate shavings, sprinkles, or a fresh strawberry slice.

4. **Serve and Enjoy:**
    - Serve these delightful Neapolitan cupcakes immediately, and enjoy the delicious combination of chocolate, vanilla, and strawberry flavors in each bite!

These Neapolitan cupcakes are sure to be a hit at parties, birthdays, or any special occasion. The layers of flavors and colors make them visually appealing, while the different frostings add a creamy and decadent finish to each cupcake.